LENIN: A SOLDIER

A Story of Survival

LENIN PATINO

BOOKSIDE Press

BOOKSIDE Press

BookSide Press
877-741-8091
www.booksidepress.com
orders@booksidepress.com

Contents

Chapter One

Before The Beginning

My name is Lenin, however I'm not the famous communist leader, but don't stop reading because this is a fascinating story as well. My full name is Lenin Patino and the book you're about to read is a true story about an unbelievable series of events and how they transformed my life.

The year was 1991, in a matter of months I would be graduating from John H. Francis Polytechnic high school in Sun Valley, California but I was unclear about what I was going do afterward. I wanted to continue with my education and play collegiate sports, but it would not be easy seeing as how the job market was not very good, and due to numerous reasons especially the lack of effort on my part I had not been recruited by any college programs and my grades were not good enough to get an academic scholarship like I always thought I would.

Complicating matters more was the fact that my parents' financial situation was not in the best shape. Fully aware of this I didn't want to burden them with helping me pay my way through college, as this would put additional pressure on their already strenuous financial situation. The Persian Gulf War had ended not too long before and the probability of any more military conflicts arising seemed to be minimal at least for quite some time.

Seeing how I had not put in any effort college entrance was going to be a lot tougher than I had originally thought, and all of the military branches were recruiting me anyway due to the fact I had scored very well on the **A.S.V.A.B.** (the vocational aptitude test given to see what careers you qualify for in the military,) and was qualified for almost any military career I wanted. I decided to take a look at what they had to offer and consider a military career instead of pursuing my education at this time.

Although not my top choice serving in the Armed Forces was something that appealed to me. In the most part because it was honorable, patriotic, and adventurous, but also for its physical and disciplinary demand. A significant number of my friends had already signed some kind of contract with one of the military branches; I would look into it as well.

I started to meet with the recruiting officers both on campus and in their respective offices or on the weekends at off campus recruiting events. First of all, I met with the Marine Corps' recruiting officer a couple of times. He told me about a lot of options in the Marines, but none of them really got my attention. I still had numerous options to explore, and seeing how I still had a few months to decide I would take a good look at the rest of my options. I met with the recruiting officers from the other branches, and some representatives from local colleges and universities. I would take my time to think about all my options and not rush my decision. I met with the Navy's recruiting officer next; he on the other hand, did get my attention with a couple of programs he told me about. First, there was the Nuclear Engineering program, which was also the option that one of my best friends at the time had chosen. Steve had already been in this particular program for over a year and seemed to be happy with his decision. In this program the moment you signed up you were automatically an E-2 and after six months of training if you signed a two-year extension, you were automatically promoted to E-4. The problem with this program was that it was a minimum six-year contract without signing the two-year extension. And I wasn't looking to make a very long career out of the Military. I just wanted to serve my country for the time on the contract, which would hopefully be short. Get some money for college then get out of the service. This way I could go back to school and possibly play collegiate sports without having to ask my parents for financial help. The second option that interested me about the Navy was the SEAL program. This to those of you who've never heard of the SEALs they are one of the top special operations force groups in the world. The only problem with this program was that it too had a minimum contract time of six years or else this would have been an option I would have loved.

Then came the meeting with the Air Force recruiting officer, this was the military branch I was most interested in since one of my biggest aspirations at the moment was to be a fighter pilot. In our first meeting I basically told the recruiting officer what I was looking for and she told me about a couple of options that got my attention, but then came the follow up meeting and the big disagreement. Despite being undersized at almost 5 feet 7 inches I participated in competitive sports my entire life and always enjoyed great amounts of success and enjoyed myself doing it. Naturally, I wanted to continue to participate in them after high school but when I asked this recruiting officer for options about participating in sports while in the Air Force, she told me to forget it because I didn't have a chance due to my lack of size. This comment really pissed me off as I felt that this was none of her business and she should just stick to doing her job as a recruiting officer not an athletic scout and there was no further contact between her and I. At this time I was pretty disillusioned about the military, so I met with a few more college representatives and intensified my job search. Eventually, I signed a tentative agreement to study electrical engineering at a nearby university. Nonetheless, I would still consider meeting with the Army's recruiting officer, this would be the final branch; However the Army was the military branch which least called my attention so I was a little reluctant to meet with them because I figured it would be a waste of my time. But the word around campus was that they had a pretty cool recruiting officer who was also a real pushover. I didn't know him at the time, even though I had seen him a lot on campus talking with some of my friends and other students.

He looked like an ogre, but when we spoke for the first time, he was actually rather pleasant, and easy to get along with. His name was Eugene Presta, he was a Staff Sergeant.

After I told him more or less what I was looking to get out of the military (a contract that was going to enable me to pay me while I was in and get money for college when I got out in at most 3 years) he told me that he would look at the options available and try to get me whatever I wanted. I was used to hearing this by now, since that is what all the recruiting officers had told me, but it turns out he wasn't like the others; Instead he seemed a lot more credible, and a much better listener. I decided to continue meeting with him and listen to what he and the Army had to offer.

A few days after I told him I might be interested in joining the Army, he approached me about an option which only had a two year contract once you got out of training which lasted about four months. It was to be Cannon Crewman also known as a 13 Bravo MOS (Military Occupational specialty) and once it finished I would get money for college through the Army college fund as well as the Montgomery G.I bill. We met a few more times so I could listen to a couple of other options and although not completely satisfied with this option, none of the others offered me what I was looking for quite like this one. 20 It was short, simple, and in addition it would get me the money for college the quickest, it would allow me to start college at 20. This was more or less what I was looking for so there were several more meetings between sergeant Presta and I to formalize the contract and its conditions. The contract said I would do all my training at Fort Sill Oklahoma and also that I would start training at the beginning of September. There were also a couple of meetings at his office to fill out paperwork. Besides these meetings there was also a trip to the downtown Los Angeles Military processing station very early in the morning. He picked me up at my house at about 3:00 am, This was for the physical exam, which was a complex exam, so they split it up into a series of stations with different doctors. To name just a few there was one station at which they would examine our sight, and hearing, another where they would examine our heart and blood pressure, yet another would test our joint movement, and muscle strength, and at another station they would look at our teeth.

Finally, as if those weren't enough there was the drug test in which we had to urinate into a small cup while some one was watching to verify that it was our urine going into the cup, this was probably the funniest and most difficult part for a good number of the people taking the physical. See there were hundreds of us thus they split us up into several groups of about fifteen. While one group was at one station the others were supposed to be at another. The big problem with this method and the reason I say the drug test was the funniest or most complicated part is because most of us had left our houses with a full bladder and to make matters worse had something to drink on our way downtown. A lot of us had to urinate all at once and there were not enough supervising officers to watch each one of us, and the drug test had to be witnessed by one of them in order for it to be official. In the meantime we were supposed to be with our groups at their respective stations but for some of us such as myself the need to go to the bathroom got so intense we didn't care whether or not it was official, and just went to the bathroom. We did not realize or care that in order for us to finish our physical we had to take this drug test with someone watching. Now it was time to go to the drinking fountain and drink as much water as you could, then wait until you had to urinate again and call someone to supervise you at the time you were going, if not you would have to do it all over again. Some of us had to urinate two or three times before we finally got someone to supervise us and make the test official. When we were finally through at least we could be assured we had some of the cleanest urinary systems around. Furthermore, I had braces and when they examined my teeth, they told me I had to have them removed by the time I was to leave for training, this might have been a problem seeing how my treatment was not even halfway completed. Time kept on ticking. I graduated at the end of June and even though I wasn't 100% pleased about having enlisted with the Army I cancelled my enrollment in the University I had signed up to go to.

Over the course of summer I took care of some things, which included prying my braces off with pliers, and other objects. Since my orthodontist had not been willing or able to take them off in a timely manner and I wasn't about to bother waiting until he felt like it. Of course neither my mom nor the orthodontist was so happy with my decision to remove my braces, but they would have to understand that it was something I had to do. During the summer I also took a trip to Honolulu, Hawaii for a week where I had a great time. Summertime flew by, September was almost here, and it would soon be time to leave for training and although I had told my girlfriend Amber I was going to the Army, I hadn't told her exactly when I would be leaving in part due to the fact that she wasn't too happy about me going into the Army. Finally, it was now early September and although still scorching hot, summer was for the most part over. A couple of days before I was scheduled to leave I showed up at Amber's house wearing a baseball cap and after a few minutes of her begging me to take it off I gave in and told her to take it off. As she pulled it off, she let out a loud scream and began to cry as she saw I had shaved my head like I had told her I would do a few days before leaving for training. On the day I was to leave I agreed to be picked up at my house by sergeant Presta just before 3:00 pm. I was a few minutes late because I was saying bye to my girlfriend and some close friends. After a few more minutes of saying goodbye to my family we got in the van and drove off. As we left, my mom was in tears asking me not to go, but we both knew that I had to. We would leave my house at about 3:15 that afternoon even though we had intended to leave by 3:00 so we would not have to put up with traffic. We would then go pick up someone else he or his partner had recruited that lived on the way to where we were going. After sitting in a nightmarish traffic jam only seen on the freeways of L.A for about thirty minutes without moving a single inch I was having second thoughts and contemplated getting out of the van and walking home. After traffic cleared up sergeant Presta took us to a hotel in downtown Los Angeles where we would then spend the rest of the afternoon finishing and verifying our enlistment paperwork, which seemed endless, and other requirements which included checking to see if I had gotten my braces off. Once again there were hundreds of us as this included all of the military recruits from all the branches in all of the Los Angeles area leaving for training that day. It took a couple of hours to finish going over the paperwork. We were then broken up into groups according to where we were going, told we would spend the night there and ship out in the morning. Each one of us was handed a voucher to go eat dinner at a nearby restaurant, assigned a room, and given a curfew of 10 pm. Most of us went walking around looking for a phone before going to eat. At Dinner I met a couple of guys that I got along pretty good with. First, there was John Bogart from somewhere in Anaheim, which is about an hour from the San Fernando Valley where I had lived most of my life. John seemed to be really easygoing, and a little quieter than the people I used to hang out with but still a great guy. Then it was Julio Beltran from Van Nuys, which is in the San Fernando Valley and just about ten minutes from Arleta the city where I had lived for the past six years. Julio and I got along great, it was as if we had been friends all of our lives when in fact we had just met. After dinner, which was wonderful, we all called home to let our families know what was going on and went back to the hotel. It was a long night as most of us were too excited and nervous to fall asleep early and stayed up until late getting to know each other. It turned out that Julio and I had grown up in some of the same places, liked some of the same activities such as skateboarding, and playing sports for our respective high schools. Curiously we had even played football against each other a couple of years earlier. The following day we woke up before the crack of dawn got sworn in and were taken to the airport. By this time John, Julio, and myself knew we were going to the same base, but we had no idea what else would happen in the next four months. The flight was a few hours long, so we slept all the way trying to make up for the lack of sleep the night before. On the way to Oklahoma we stopped in Denver for fuel. Since our stay here was not going to be too long we weren't allowed to get off the plane. Finally we got to the airport in Oklahoma City, Oklahoma where after picking up our baggage we would catch a bus for a couple of hours to Lawton, a small town just outside the base. Once in Lawton we took a van into Fort Sill.

We were all surprised when we first got there, seeing how they didn't treat us as badly as we all anticipated. This was the reception station where they would teach us a few basic things such as how to properly:

- Make our beds
- Shine our boots
- Address superior officers and drill Sergeants
- March
- Do push-ups

Here they would also confiscate contraband articles such as pocketknives, and other dangerous items we weren't supposed to have. The driver of the van pointed out a small group of drill Sergeants when we were first brought into the base, and they looked like walking GI Joe action figures. These drill Sergeants were all tall and muscular, their uniforms were perfect. The shirt and pants looked as crisp as humanly possible as if they had just been dry-cleaned or ironed. Their boots were tremendously shiny and wore a big round campaign hat that not only complemented their uniform which as the driver told us was their symbol of pride that set them apart from anyone else. Despite their uniform's splendor they looked extremely mean and despite everyone here treating us somewhat well so far we were still afraid to mess up the beds that night seeing how none of us knew how to make them up again at least not to meet their standards. That first night some of us including me slept on top of the covers, so that it was only a matter of tightening them up the following morning, not that

I managed to get too much sleep that night seeing how there were artillery explosions all night. Although it was still summer it was cooler than a normal summer night I also almost froze that night, as I'm sure everyone else that did not unmake their bed almost did as well, but sleeping on top of the covers was better than having to put up with a screaming drill Sergeant in your face the next day. This was the routine until about the third day when Corporal Drummonds (a drill Sergeant in training) showed us how to properly make a bed. Another thing they did here was issue us our uniforms and other important gear. They also taught us how to get in and out of formation, how to enter the mess hall, which is what the military calls, the restaurant, and how to use some of our equipment. Perhaps the most important thing they did here was get us somewhat used to the schedule of waking up before 6:00 am and as one of the drill Sergeants there put it "get more done by 10:00 am than most people do all day." Here we would also learn a very common practice in the Army "Hurry up and wait"

I believe it was on the fourth day or that everyone had to get a haircut and it was off to the barber, even though I didn't have any hair I had to go with them. There were some depressing sights that day, there were some guys in the group that had been letting their hair grow for a couple of years and in fact it looked healthy I would say nice, but I personally don't like long hair. Some of these guys watched in disbelief and almost cried as their curls came tumbling down. Then it was off to see the doctor or medics so that they could give each one of us the required shots and exams. There were many different injections, so we had to go there on two different occasions in order to get all of them. We stayed in the reception station about a week while we were through with in processing and had been issued all of the necessary uniforms, and gear.

Once they saw we were all in processed and had all the necessary knowledge and equipment needed for training; they called the training facility so they could send for us. The same day in the afternoon a cattle wagon picked us up and took us across the train tracks and into ``Drill Sergeant territory´´ as the area where the training facilities are located is known. It was an unbelievably hot, and stormy day there were close to fifty of us each one carrying a rucksack or backpack full of camping equipment, a pair of oversized duffel bags with more gear and uniforms, and one maybe two bags with our personal stuff. As you can probably imagine we were packed in tighter than Sardines in a can, on top of that it was raining so we had our wet gear on, which made it feel even hotter. As if that wasn't enough, they sent a few drill Sergeants that had a face only a mother could love. First of all, there was drill Sergeant Johnson who was the worst because he was always furiously yelling. I guess this was either due to the fact that he had a lot of combat experience and probably thought was always in combat fighting for his life or he was supposed to intimidate us and was very good at his job. Another drill Sergeant who was not so bad, was drill Sergeant Taylor, he looked to be barely older than most of us and had a voice like a character in a Disney movie. He also yelled a lot and did so with a deep tone in order to disguise his whiney voice and make it sound intimidating he tried to but it often cracked giving us some much needed humor. Last but not least, someone had to drive; this was drill Sergeant Morgan's job. We did not see him very much, but we quickly noticed that he looked very much like a Bulldog. Although he appeared to be mellower, and more even-tempered than the other two, we soon realized he was still a drill Sergeant, and his job was to yell and give us a hard time. We struggled to get situated in the truck and immediately after we were all on the truck, it started moving even though we weren't all set yet. This caused chaos as we bumped into each other and some of us even fell. Finally, after we had all gotten set and were the most comfortable, we would be while on the truck the vehicle came to a sudden stop in the middle of an open field and the drill Sergeants told us to get off because they needed to teach us some very important commands. Although they did instruct us on a couple of procedures used when falling into formation they were a review of some commands that we had learned while we were at the reception station. Reviewing them did not seem to be anything that important that couldn't have waited until we got to our final destination. Apparently all they wanted to do was make life more difficult for us by making us get out in the middle of the rain and get all wet, and muddy. Before they made us get on again they had us do some push-ups in the middle of the flooded field, then it was time to get back on the truck.

This time seeing as our boots and hands were full of mud it was more complicated to get on, and almost comfortable again. What is amazing to me is how with their mere presence and voices the three of them controlled almost fifty of us. It was off to our unit the entire ride was extremely bumpy causing us to bounce from one side to another and into the hard unforgiving steel. The only way to avoid falling was to be in a corner squished by all your bags.

Not including the nearly twenty minutes we were in the middle of the muddy field the ride had lasted about an hour by my calculations and, had left us pretty banged up so we were quite happy when we stopped again, and the drill Sergeants told us we were at our unit C battery 1/33FA Once there they really began to treat us like a pack of wild animals. While we were still in the truck squishing each other they relentlessly yelled at us for almost a half an hour. By this time we all felt like getting out and running, but I think if we had known what was waiting for us outside the truck all of us would have stayed in the truck no matter how uncomfortable. When they finally made us get down it was a rude awakening, no more nice guys here. It looked and felt like they had gotten all the drill Sergeants in the Army to come yell at us the drill Sergeants outnumbered the recruits by at the very least a 2-to1 ratio it was unbelievable. When we finally got out of the truck we had to sprint about the length of a football field with all of that baggage and with what seemed to be at least 300 Neanderthal men constantly yelling at us to go faster and to keep our bags up. Then we had to fall into formation and hold our bags up until they finished yelling. We were supposed to be looking straight ahead and hardly even breathing. Everywhere you turned there were at least two drill Sergeants staring in your face and vigorously yelling each one had veins popping out of their necks and faces looking like they were going to explode. Yelling at each one of us even if we had done nothing wrong seemed to motivate them to yell more. After about twenty minutes of standing in formation they told us to run upstairs without letting the bags drag, or else we would have to do it all over again. I don't even know how we did it, in most cases we had two or three bags in each hand and as if that was not tough enough we also had bags hanging from our necks, mouths,. Finally, after a long struggle we all managed to get upstairs and into the barracks which would be our home for the next seventeen weeks. Upstairs there were only three drill Sergeants who were waiting to see who came up and how.

Once everyone was upstairs one of them told us to get into formation. Then drill Sergeant Johnson yelled at us some more. Eventually, they lined us up and told us to go beside the beds and set our bags down beside the one we were being assigned. There were a couple of guys dragging their bags to where they had to go. These guys were automatically assigned to the Floor crew and had to go downstairs and come back up carrying all of their bags.

That first night we filled out more papers while kneeling by our beds and taking a break every once in a while to do pushups and get punished in other ways. I personally preferred this punishment to being on my knees, which felt like they were being crushed. We did this until about midnight. It was probably the most awful night I had ever had, and I seriously doubt that anyone in the group would argue with that. There were some members of my platoon that even cried that night when drill Sergeant Johnson was yelling at them, but they quickly confronted the situation stopped crying and began doing what they were supposed to do. After all no one had forced them to join. The three drill Sergeants that were upstairs would be our platoon's drill Sergeants for the entire duration of training. Fortunately for us in the next couple of days there were many new recruits coming in so they had to make another platoon. This meant that drill Sergeant Johnson could not be with us for the remainder of training, because he had to take charge of the new platoon. Of course we were all heartbroken over this. Instead of three we had only two drill Sergeants. Which were more than enough for us First of all, there was drill Sergeant Musselwhite who was our platoon Sergeant, he was an airborne Ranger and always excelled at just about everything he did and expected us to do the same. With this way of thinking he immediately put the pressure on us to be the best platoon of the cycle. Then there was drill Sergeant Mayfield who was our assistant platoon Sergeant, and also put a lot of pressure on us to be the best. He was not an airborne Ranger, but he was also a bad ass, he had been in an air rescue squad in Dessert Storm I got along better with him. At least to me he seemed a lot easier to relate to, seeing as he was more approachable probably because he was younger, and apparently not there every day so when he was there he seemed to be in a descent mood. Besides he seemed to be interested in some of the same things we were. Of course there were people that preferred drill Sergeant Musselwhite.

Chapter Two

Learning the Basics

On September 11th, 1992, Basic training officially began, we were awakened extremely early, placed into different squads according to the bed that we had been assigned to just a few hours earlier. To my surprise I looked to the right and a couple of beds down it was John Bogart, then I looked to my left and in the bed right beside me was Julio Beltran. Each Squad was assigned areas of the barracks to keep clean. My squad, which was 1st squad, was assigned to the bathrooms, 2nd squad the windows, and the recreation room, 3rd squad the laundry room and downstairs platoon area, and 4th Squad were assigned the floor, and staircase. The people that dragged their bags the night before besides being put into a separate squad were also assigned to help with the floor. Their main task, however, was to keep the floor shining like a mirror especially the front of the barracks. Seeing as how it was the most important area in the barracks and if it was not up to expectations we all got yelled at none of us had any problem with helping out by waxing and buffing the floor during our turns at guard and free time. Actually I shouldn't say, "we didn't have any problem" since it was more like we didn't have any choice. We were the second platoon Raiders, and even though not all of us got along very well we helped each other out on just about everything. As you can imagine it was not easy living with more than forty total strangers for more than four months. Our training period was a lot longer than we had all expected. Our training was not like normal basic training where you are at one base for four weeks then you get to go home before you go somewhere else to complete your (A.I.T) job training instead in O.S.U.T (One Station Unit Training) we were stuck in one base for the entire four month period. I think that by the end of training even the drill Sergeants were tired of yelling at the same people. Training went along on schedule but not without its fair share of memorable and not so memorable events. The first few weeks were calm despite being the toughest because everyone was just getting used to a lot of things including each other, the gear, especially the boots, which were extremely uncomfortable. During these first couple of weeks we also had to endure and get used to the physical and psychological maltreatment and domination. We were being put through. They had to indoctrinate us, and the easiest way was to tear us down to zero and build us up again. There were some guys that just could not handle it and were placed on suicide watch, which basically consisted of taking away their shoelaces, belts, and anything else, they could use to commit suicide with. A few others had to be sent home due to their inability to cope. Despite all these factors the first few weeks were pretty quiet in fact the events that most come to mind from these was our first and shortest road march which was only one and a half miles long, but seemed to be the longest one as we were not used to the boots and seemed like if it took forever. There was also the day that the drill Sergeants asked for a few volunteers to go on a detail with a few drill Sergeants including drill Sergeant Johnson. I thought, "Now how hard can this be, it's probably something dumb and easy." So I volunteered along with a few other guys. It was something dumb, but it was not very easy, as it consisted of walking along the highway picking up all the trash people had thrown out of their cars. We had to do this for about five miles with the sun beaming down on our heads, and the drill Sergeants right on our butts, about the most memorable thing in the first month was a time some guy named Masengill and I had gotten in trouble for some reason or another and one weekend while the rest of the platoon went on pass for a few hours we had to stay behind and dig a trench. When we were about halfway done digging we were told that we could go eat lunch so we headed to the mess hall where there was an enormous wait, eventually we got our food, and in order to get some rest ate as slowly as we could, this was the most enjoyable meal I had had since arriving at Fort Sill. When we got outside we saw that the weather had dramatically changed while we were eating lunch, in the time we were inside it had gone from being a blistering sunny morning to a windy, rainy dark afternoon. We were feeling good as this might help soften the concrete like dirt we had to dig the trench in. While we were walking towards the field it started raining harder and harder in fact the closer we got the harder it rained. It turns out that what we thought was good turned out to be a disaster, it had rained so hard that it washed out the portion of trench we had already dug so after almost crying we had to start shoveling dirt out all over again. The good thing was that this time it was softer dirt. Even with the dirt as soft as mud it still took us a couple of hours to finish as you might expect all of training was not quite so uneventful as a matter of fact it seemed that every time we turned around we were getting yelled at or being dusted (punished). On rare occasions because we had actually done something wrong most of the time it was just because that was part of training. We got dusted because we ate too slowly, walked too slow, or turned our heads in line etc. regardless of why it seems like if we were always doing push-ups, sit-ups, jumping- jacks, or running. There were times that a drill Sergeant would wake us up in the middle of the night and have us go downstairs and made us run a few miles before breakfast only to have us run more after breakfast. Typically this was done to individual platoons by one of their platoon Sergeants; in my battery there were four platoons. Every platoon had at least two drill Sergeants, and if that wasn't enough there was a senior drill Sergeant Sergeant Lee, a first Sergeant Sergeant Bankster and a unit commanding officer Captain

Quintero plus the drill Sergeants from other units any of which would punish us at any time for anything. On many occasions the four platoons were also punished together as one big group we all lined up in the same battery area, which was a big courtyard with four distinct platoon areas, barracks, and laundry rooms. It was like an apartment complex only that instead of parking spaces they used the space below the buildings for platoon areas. When we lined up we could all see each other I recall one morning after breakfast we were lined up as a battery and drill Sergeant Taylor who was fourth platoon's drill Sergeant went up to their barracks saw a few beds that were not made to his satisfaction. He was so angry we all heard as he yelled and flipped beds, then he opened a window threw a few mattresses out and came down and dusted everyone while lecturing us about neatness and following orders. His platoon, for that matter the entire battery was terrified. In the neighboring courtyards other units were also going through the same hell we were some had started their basic training before us while others had just gotten there. Regardless of how long any of us had been there we recruits were treated like the lowest form of life on the entire planet. We would often run into these other units as we marched to and from the mess hall or ran around the base. Many times the four platoons were given physical Training by drill Sergeant Mayfield whose regimen always included making us run a few miles as fast as he did and he was a great runner. We had heard from the other drill Sergeants that he was the best running drill Sergeant on the base. He usually had us run four miles in about thirty minutes at least twice a week. We would practically sprint the first, slow down slightly for the second and third then once again pick up the pace for the final mile only to dust us some more in the courtyard. Some just could not keep up and came in well back it might have been the toughest thing in basic training. On one of these runs we ran by this other unit that was running with a few drill Sergeants from their battery we were both a few miles away from our battery areas which were right next to each other so the drill Sergeants agreed that it would be fun and competitive to see who could run back to their respective battery area and get in battery formation first. So they told us what the plan was and some of the drill Sergeants left to go see who got there first we had to wait about twenty minutes for the drill Sergeants that stayed to tell us to go. In this time there was a lot of trash talking. When they finally told us to go there was a good amount of pushing and shoving there were some punches thrown and a few guys got knocked down. In the hurry to get back first tempers flared but it didn't amount to much just then because we were all too interested in getting back first after all somebody had to win. Well it was a good run we cheered for our friends and our enemies alike. Finally after everyone in our battery was lined up drill Sergeant Lee was going to do a head count to make sure everyone was there before radioing the other unit to let them know we had won when a guy from our platoon came walking into the Battery area. As every one of us yelled for him to line up despite having flat feet and being exhausted he started to give it his best effort to run and get in formation but just as he was getting into our platoon area a drill Sergeant from the other unit radioed drill Sergeant Lee to check on our progress and let him know that his battery was all lined up. Even though it wasn't by much we had lost. Well it was time for breakfast we went as a battery and passed by the same unit on our way to the mess hall. There was so much anger that we were going to fight right then and there. Their drill Sergeants saw what could happen and to avoid problems took them around another way. However when we got to the mess hall you guessed it; they were right in front of us in line. So once again the trash talking started right up and tempers began to flare then their last man in line decided to go ahead and punch our platoon guide in the head that is when all of us immediately rushed up ready to fight even the other platoons were trying to help Us. The fight did not last as the drill Sergeants broke it all up before it got completely out of control. Then they took their respective units back to their battery area and dusted us all before letting us go to breakfast. Immediately after breakfast we got in formation as we usually did to go back to our battery area we waited for a drill Sergeant to come give us the order to go back. The other unit was in formation doing the same right in front of us. They looked like we felt. Despite having significant distance between us the trash talking had started start up again. When we were about to start fighting all the drill Sergeants just appeared out of nowhere. Everyone immediately quieted down then the drill Sergeants dusted the other unit until just about everyone had thrown up what they had eaten. Of course, we enjoyed seeing this and were all giggling and making fun of the other unit, but our joy wouldn't last very long seeing as how we were next. Then they punished us like we had never been punished before and would never be punished again in the rest of training. In fact most if not all of my Battery also threw up that morning. Funny thing is that after this the rest of training went along without any major incidents. We started to get along better and didn't have as many arguments at least between members of the same platoon, and seemed to be somewhat more united even though we still did not get along with everyone. In basic training we were issued an M16 we were taught how to shoot and clean our weapons, we also learned how to shoot a rocket launcher, a 50-caliber machine gun, how to set and detonate claymore mines, and how to safely arm and throw grenades of course this was tough as none of us had ever been around weapons of this magnitude. Other things we learned included First aid, map reading and how to read a compass, as well as what to do in case of a Biological, Nuclear or Chemical attack we even had to clean our weapons with all this gear on. It was the same as cleaning it without it only that on that day it was extremely hot and since we had our normal uniforms plus chemical suits which included a Gas mask on it seemed even hotter. As part of the Biological Nuclear Chemical training, we also had to endure the Gas Chamber in which we had to go into a room as a platoon stood against the walls while drill Sergeants came by and checked that our masks were working properly. Then the room filled with tear gas. Two at a time we had to go up to the drill Sergeant that was there say our rank, unit, and ID number then place our Gas mask on before going out. In the days prior to the Gas Chamber I recall drill Sergeant Mayfield telling us that it was nothing that he would even go in and do some push- ups inside and he did. We also learned how to repel down a mountain side, how to set up the area where the cannons were going to be placed this included measuring coordinates to park the cannons and setting up radio communications, of course we had to learn the basics of how to load the projectiles into the cannons which included matching up the correct projectile with the appropriate fuse as well as the gunpowder that would launch it. Perhaps the most exciting thing we did was an obstacle course where we had to crawl through a four foot high concrete pipe, climb over a six foot wall, then dive into a muddy trench and drag ourselves a length of about twenty feet while keeping low because the trench was covered by barb wire. Later in the course we had to cross a bridge made of three steel ropes one to walk on while holding on to the others. Finally after we were all exhausted we had to cross a small creek by sliding across a rope about ten feet above it. I'm not sure how many of us made it but I don't think it was too many, I know I fell into the water when one of my gloves slipped off. When we got back to the barracks after hosing off most of the mud we had to wash the entire courtyard and laundry room prior to going upstairs and changing into a clean uniform before going to dinner.

Then we started to get ready for the biggest and toughest inspection of training. In this final inspection some of the base commanders would come and inspect the barracks and all of our gear, which besides being spotless had to be precisely laid out on the beds, there were too many requirements to remember but I remember that when we were done setting up if you stooped down at one end and looked across the row of beds they were uniformly lined up so that you could only see one of each item. At approximately the same time we were learning how to march with weapons, we practiced two or more hours every day until we perfected our routine then we practiced some more. At the beginning of training we were asked if there were preferences in regard to where we were sent so I put Hawaii and California as my first two choices. Not that it mattered much as when we received our orders, which told us our first regular duty Stations would be. I believe that not many of us got either of their choices. Most of the unit stayed stationed at Fort Sill, while others were sent to bases around the country I along with a few others got stationed at Fort Riley Kansas. Not that anyone was complaining but for some unknown reason just in time for Christmas training was over and we got to go back home before we had to go off to our regular duty station. Sure basic training was tough at times, but it was not as bad as it sounds. After all I got to meet guys from all over the country, with different cultures, interests, and upbringings, some of us practiced sports others were real good students and others were involved in gangs and sold drugs as well. Somehow though we pulled together and managed to survive. When I arrived at Fort Riley in January of 1993 it was freezing and the road into the base had lots of accumulated snow, the buildings had icicles hanging down from the sides of the roofs, the first night I was part of a small group that had to spend the night in some place in the outskirts of the base called Camp Forsythe in a cabin that looked and felt like if it had been built in World War I not World War II like we were told. The following day we were transferred to a newer building inside the main base where we would spend one or two days inprocessing before being transferred to our regular unit. There I met up with John Rodriguez a soldier/friend I had been in basic training with. John and I would end up in adjacent buildings seeing how we were both assigned to the same battalion only that he was in Bravo Battery, and I was assigned to the Headquarters Battery, which was a very important Battery. This unit required special security clearance that only United States citizens were allowed to have and since I was not born in the US I did not have, after a few days they realized that I wasn't a Citizen, so I was transferred to Alpha battery which I kind of wanted since I had heard that being on the line in one of the units with the cannons was a faster way to go up rank. I was quickly overwhelmed by the weather conditions, in the daytime temperatures were always close to or below zero, at night the wind would usually blow and made it seem even colder. When it snowed, which was quite often the snow would get packed down and freeze in a matter of hours. People including me would often slip and fall especially when we were in a hurry to get somewhere. I must have fallen at least a hundred times in the first two weeks alone. Once I was transferred to Alpha battery, which was in the next building over, I was placed in second platoon 7th section. Of course since I was the new guy I would be the advanced party of the section (the one that is responsible for preparing the area for the cannons to park). It was so cold that the first week I was in Alpha battery since there was no phone in the room whenever I needed to make a phone call I had to use a payphone just outside of the building. As I talked on the phone my head filled with curiosity as to how cold it really was, so one time before I went inside I spit, and it froze within seconds of hitting the ground. To make things worse whenever the wind blew there was a howling sound that traveled through my room and made it almost impossible to sleep. Unfortunately though almost every morning the whole section would get up at about 4:30 am to take a shower and go have breakfast before we did PT only to walk for about fifteen minutes to the motor pool where the Howitzers (mechanized cannons) were. At the motor pool we all cleaned up the snow that accumulated on the ground, but each section performed maintenance on their own Howitzer and parking spot After several weeks we had what was my first trip to the field, fortunately I had great colleagues who had given me lots of advice on how to do my job better. The training mission went along as planned, when we got back though we had to wash the Howitzers and other vehicles we had taken almost immediately. The best way to do so was by passing them through a canal while someone sprayed each side with a high-pressure hose in order to get all the mud off. During the washing of the vehicles we also got ourselves soaked, not by choice but by necessity. It wasn't long before we found ourselves ready preparing to go to the National Training Center at Fort Irwin California for training. I was excited because this meant that in our time off I could probably go home and visit everyone without costing me any leave time at the same time. However my excitement was short-lived, as I believe that at the same time the entire battalion was placed on standby to go to Somalia. While stationed in Kansas I made a lot of new friends both within the base and from nearby cities like Manhattan and Junction City, also on some weekends a few friends and I would go to cities that were further away like Topeka, Wichita, and a few others.

Chapter Three:

Tragedy Strikes

On the night of Friday March 19th 1993 while stationed with the 2nd platoon Alpha battery 1st of the 5th in Fort Riley Kansas I was critically wounded. The way it happened from what little I recall, what I've read and been told by others that were present is that a few hours after dinner I was in my room watching TV, and getting ready to go out when another soldier member of the same unit who was also a friend had been walking around the hall waving a handgun around showing it to everyone walked into my room and started to point the weapon jokingly threatening me, and some of the others in the room at the time. I quickly confronted him we started joking around and told him to get out and put the gun away. He then walked further into the room and said, "Why don't you make me?" At this time against better judgment I got up in his face and once again told him to put the gun away. I've been told he then pointed the gun at my head and said, "I'm going to shoot your ass." I thought that he wouldn't do it since we got along pretty well so I stupidly turned around put my arms up and responded "Do it if you got the balls." Little did I know but he had had a few drinks and shoved the gun against my head and pulled the trigger.

I immediately lost consciousness and fell to the ground as the bullet traveled through my head splattering blood and brain matter all over the room. Some of the other soldiers in the barracks including him were in panic however in the midst of the confusion almost immediately someone called for the paramedics while others rolled me out of the puddle of blood and performed first aid procedures until the paramedics got there and rushed me to the nearest medical facility totally unconscious and almost completely dead.

Next thing I knew was about three weeks later when I regained some consciousness. I opened my eyes in a cold sweat and a cold bed at Stormont-Vail a medical clinic in Topeka, Kansas. As I opened my eyes I saw my mom, my mom, my grandmother, and my Aunt Alba. While one of them hovered over me holding a wet cloth towel on my forehead they all told me that everything was going to be all right and asked if I recognized them, but otherwise they did not tell me anything about what had happened. I knew something was wrong but had no idea what it was.

Eventually I noticed that I was not able to move a finger or any part of my body except for my eyes. I had tubes, needles, and wires coming from just about every part of my body including one coming out of my nose, which was the only one I could clearly see. Despite having lost an enormous amount of blood, having severe infections which led to having extremely high fevers for a few days, and some very weak vital signs such as low blood pressure, and a slow heart rate, and not being able to move I was still able to see, hear, feel and reason. I knew exactly who I was and recognized all my family members. I wondered where I was, but it wasn't long before I realized that I was in a hospital bed but didn't know why.

I just felt like I had been unplugged. Regardless of the loud noise being made by all the machines in the room which among others included a heart monitor, a blood pressure monitor, a feeding machine which was pumping liquid formula into my stomach through the feeding tube in my nose, inflatable tube socks to help prevent blood clots from forming I heard strange voices in the background saying some things to the effect that I was not going to survive. I also noticed my family was praying over my body as if I were dead or dying.

Deep inside me somewhere I wondered what was going on. I wanted to scream but my mouth would not move my jaw was stiff and I couldn't even talk. I wanted to get up, but my body would not respond. As a matter of fact it didn't even let me try. I was trapped in my own body it was like something inside was telling me "Just lay there and let yourself die." So eventually I just stopped trying and even thinking about it.

For many days I lay in bed unconscious the majority of the time but at other times somewhat or completely conscious. During those periods of consciousness, which seemed like an eternity I would lay there powerless to voluntarily move a muscle or make a noise. For hours each and every day many thoughts went through my head but it didn't matter how hard I tried concentrating I could not think about anything in particular. It was just like my mind was trying to make some sense out of all this. Like a computer searching for a missing file on the hard drive just could not stop wandering from thought to thought trying to find something that wasn't there trying pointlessly because I came up blank every time.

With no one aware of my consciousness I did the only thing I could do at that time and that was to listen to everything that went on around me becoming like a fly on a wall, aware of everything that was being said around me but unable to express myself in any way, shape, or form.

No one on the medical staff believed I could hear them or that I knew what was going on, so they kept telling my family about how I was on my deathbed. In fact they thought I was going to die or if somehow I did pull through and manage to survive or if by some miracle I did, they thought I would never regain consciousness forcing me to live on artificial life support.

Hearing this caused me to at times feel helpless, confused, and somewhat scared, and the thought "Maybe everyone is right just let yourself die it's definitely easier, and could be better." Often passed through my mind, but either my training to survive which had been so hammered into me during the short period of time I was in the Army, or my stubbornness kicked in and just would not let me quit fighting.

As a result of the gunshot my brain or what was left of it had swollen incredibly. The bullet which had caused significant amounts of brain damage as it crossed my head also shattered the skull while exploding at its exit point leaving behind skull fragments along with bullet fragments some which I still have inside my brain as removing them would cause more damage than it would do good.

Dr. Aryunen the Neurosurgeon on the team that saved my life, in order to do so had successfully removed most the pieces of shattered skull that splintered into my brain when I was shot. Although a necessary and wonderful life -saving surgery, which I will always be extraordinarily thankful for it had some negative sides to it. Perhaps the biggest downside was that with some of the pieces of bone that he removed he also removed more brain tissue that was attached to the bone causing greater amounts of brain damage and leaving a large aperture on the upper right side of my cranium where my brain would no longer have the skull to protect it.

Now don't think it was just out in the open for all to see as it did have skin over it, but it did not have the essential added protection the skull provides. It was like a baby's soft spot only a great deal bigger. Furthermore, I had developed severe infections probably the most serious being severe Pneumonia causing complications such as extreme fevers and almost killing me. In addition, I lost incredible amounts of weight in large part due to severe muscle atrophy or shrinkage from being inactive and not able to eat for so long. My bodyweight went down to about seventy pounds, which was significantly less than half of my normal weight of close to two hundred pounds. I was practically skin draped over a skeleton or as my grandmother once told me "You looked like a cadaver."

Many outstanding medical procedures were needed to save my life; the majority of which were performed while I was completely unconscious. Doctors had obviously placed me on a respirator, performed a blood transfusion, and inserted the feeding tube through my nose, which traveled down my comatose body into my stomach. They had also performed a tracheotomy this is where they cut a hole in my trachea and left a little tube sticking out of my neck just below my Adam's apple in order for them to clean out my lungs regularly. This also meant that even if I by some means did regain consciousness my vocal cords would likely be permanently damaged and I might not ever talk right if at all again, but as you will later see this would be the least of my problems.

At times I was conscious but everyone on the medical staff thought that I was not and would never again be. In fact if you saw me I think you would have agreed with them, but I kept surprising everyone and after a couple of weeks the doctors determined that I no longer depended on the respirator to breathe, so they went ahead and removed it placing me on oxygen though since I was still in a delicate condition. By this time I was for the most part aware of everything going on, even with the large amounts of medication that was being pumped into my body, had developed a system of communicating with my family and medical staff by blinking my eyes. Blinking once meant, "Yes", and blinking twice meant "No"

I mean it wasn't much and rather difficult, but at least I could answer some "yes" and "no" questions which would make everyone aware that I still had a life and was not about to let go of it so easily. This was especially important because the doctors had already told my family that they should start considering pulling me off of the artificial life support I was on. A few days later seeing I was not getting enough nutrition and still losing a lot of weight they also removed the feeding tube from my nose and placed another feeding tube a PEG tube just above my naval and directly into my stomach.

The removal of the feeding tube from my nose caused a bit of discomfort and pain as it was pulled out of my nostril. However it was nothing compared to the pain from the opening of the hole in my stomach, which was so excruciating that I almost bit through my lips and tongue since I did not have a bite block in place. I don't know if it was that the Anesthetic that was injected did not work or if it was done before it had taken its full effect, but one thing I know is that it was the worst physical pain I had endured up to then. Soon after this day I believe they officially declared me out of the comatose condition that they had me in. Although I was now one step closer to being stable I still had a tough road ahead. Shortly after this, seeing I was out of immediate danger, and getting better my mom left, she went back home to California to be with my younger brothers. My grandmother and aunt stayed behind to be with me, I still had the tracheotomy and could not eat or drink anything yet at least not through the mouth. I did have an IV in my arm for medications and essential liquids; meanwhile another machine fed me automatically through the tube in my stomach every few hours according to doctors' orders. Since I was still in the Intensive Care Unit the nurse at the nurses' station monitored me 24 hours a day. Apart from this every few hours a nurse had to come in and check my diaper, as I had no Bowel or bladder control, I was like an 18-year-old baby, I went to the bathroom in a diaper and urinated into a bag through a urinary catheter or hose, which was inserted, into my bladder through my penis. There were also the respiratory therapists that came in periodically every few hours flipped me from side to side and pounded on my chest, and back in order to loosen the phlegm in my lungs so they could suction it out through my tracheotomy. This was when they would stick something that looked like a straw down the tube my throat and vacuum my lungs. The suction straw down my throat was tremendously unpleasant and made me cough nonstop, which just made more mucous come loose. This would go on for about five to ten minutes I believe although it felt like hours, and because of the severe discomfort and work my limp body had to do as it would shake nonstop from coughing uncontrollably and squirmed trying to stop the asphyxiating sensation. Afterwards, I would usually be exhausted and drenched in sweat. Every few hours the nurses would also disconnect me from the feeding machine in order to manually give me some much needed water which was refreshing even though it never went through my throat. They usually took this time to wiggle the feeding tube and clear the scab from the area around it so it would not develop an infection this was also tremendously painful and uncomfortable as it generally felt like they were pulling my guts out.

Over the next few weeks as the swelling in my brain went down my medical condition became more stable, and I became more and more aware. Finally I began to weakly move my right index finger and then the right middle finger. At this time I saw doctors were amazed with my progress and more and more of them came to see me every morning on their rounds. They asked questions, although they tried to make them all simple "yes and "No" questions so I could answer by putting up one finger for "yes" and two fingers for "No." This new system was a lot clearer and easier to communicate with than blinking my eyes.

Eventually as the swelling in the brain went down and with lots of hard work by my family, the medical staff, and myself I would regain movement of all my fingers and most range of motion in my right arm. It was weak but at least it moved

Although the doctors and the rest of the medical staff were all astonished with my recovery and very excited to see me move my arm they did not want me to hurt myself. Seeing how I still had many hoses and wires attached to my body I was very curious and was always pulling at all the cables and wires especially the hose which I would urinate through since it was extremely bothersome, I would also throw my hand in the direction of the tracheotomy and pull some of the tubes around my neck one of which delivered oxygen and medicine to my lungs. Eventually they tied my hand to the railing on the bed untying it only during therapy sessions or when they needed to turn me over for some reason or another, and then tied it again immediately after they were done. Over the next couple of weeks there were Urine tests, X-rays, blood tests, and physical therapy sessions practically every day. I was so sick of just lying there but there was nothing anybody could do.

I was tremendously fortunate seeing as the members of the medical staff were very friendly, knowledgeable and perhaps best of all, most of them were beautiful young women whom I would somehow flirt and play games with every time I could. While they had me on my left side facing them this included putting my arm around their waist grabbing their butts and, at other times, taking their pens out of their pockets and dropping them to the ground. I don't know why I would get such a big kick out of this, but I thought it was hilarious watching them bend over and pick them up, not to mention that most had nice looking butts. I was like a kid in a candy store besides most of them didn't seem to mind or if they did they certainly didn't show it. On the other hand my

41

grandma did, and she would always let me know by either looking at me with a real nasty look on her face or just straight out telling me that it wasn't right. My favorite time of day was probably Physical Therapy with Jeff seeing as he made me laugh a lot even though no sound was made by me I felt like I was laughing. Some of the laughter was from the pain caused by the stretches and exercises we would do, but most of it was because he just made me laugh with the stuff he said and did. Our session was only about an hour long, but we would spend at least 45 minutes of this time laughing as we worked, he was the first person I remember to take off my oxygen for even a few moments, he would also ask me addition questions like "what is 2+2?" To test me and I would put up the right number of fingers every time. Soon he would ask me to answer some questions with the answer being numbers with double digits thinking I might not be able to do it but I surprised him and opened and shut my fingers to show him the correct answer. One day he asked me some question I knew the answer to but could not answer him by using my fingers, so I stuck my middle finger out. He thought this was hilarious and started cracking up I laughed with him but no sound would come out. He laughed so loud that everyone on the ward including my aunt, and grandma who had been drinking coffee down the hall came running in to see if there was something wrong. When he explained most of the nurses thought it was funny too and kept asking me similar questions. There was also the time that he was going to perform stretch on my leg by picking it up and in the middle of the stretch noticed I had a dirty diaper and poop had oozed out all over the bed and all over my leg we thought this was especially funny and laughed for a while I laughed so hard it hurt. He then called in a nurse that would clean me up so we could continue. Jeff would not let me forget it because every other time before he started a session the first thing he would do was make a joke about it then ask me if I needed to be changed and check my diaper.

There were also the times that they weighed me. First of all, they would bring in a machine that looked like a hammock on a meat scale with a car jack attached to it. They would roll me out of the way and then place it on the mattress and roll me from side to side until I was completely centered on a cloth in the middle of two steel bars which would always dig into the little meat I had when I was being rolled over them, sometimes colliding with my bones causing lots of discomfort and pain. Finally they would pump it up until it was totally clear off of the bed and read the weight, meanwhile I felt like the catch of the day. From all the pulling I would do whenever my arm was tied to the bedrails I had regained some muscle tone and strength mostly in my biceps, shoulder, and triceps, as these were the muscles I used to pull against the strap. I don't know how but doing this also strengthened my fingers and the whole right side of my trunk and upper body.

During the time I spent at Stormont-Vail, which is a couple of hours away from the Fort Riley area, where I had most of my military friends, and a lifetime away from my family, some of them really surprised me by either calling or visiting me. Although I could not talk I did receive frequent phone calls, when someone called either a nurse or a family member would hold the handset up to my ear and the people would talk to me. I could feel the joy as my face lit up with happiness whenever I heard a familiar voice especially when it was my girlfriends'. I also received a few surprising visitors, some of my friends came in the first couple of days after the gunshot so I don't remember who, but somehow know they were there. On the other hand there were some whom I remember very well including two beautiful young women who really cheered up my day every time they came to see me, which was every few days. One of them was my friend Michelle whom I used to see whenever I went dancing, which I did often and although she surprised me perhaps more surprisingly was her friend Shauna whom I really did not know but always went with Michelle. Eventually as my condition improved I was transferred from Stormont-Vail to Irwin community hospital the military clinic inside Fort Riley. It was a sad day for me because I had developed a good relationship with most of the medical staff at Stormont-Vail and would have to start over with new people and a new system. Of course this would also put me closer and more accessible to my military colleagues, and friends. I was transported by ambulance. It was a new experience since it was my first trip in an ambulance at least while I was conscious. Even though I was conscious at the time I remember very little about the long ambulance ride as I could not see much

44

except the inside of the Ambulance and what I was able to see through one of the windows which wasn't much. There was a big problem when I first arrived at Irwin Community as they did not have the feeding machine that I required and the doctor that initially received me was telling my aunt that it was no big deal, but I had a terrible headache, a stomach ache and everything else you can think off caused by hunger as I had not been fed for well over 24 hours My aunt quickly realized that she was not going to get anywhere arguing with him went and somehow spoke with the person running the hospital, and several of the base commanding officers, that same night Lieutenant Colonel Hill my Battery Commanding officer personally came to see me, and soon after he arrived the feeding machine did as well. I spent a few weeks here, but it seemed a lot longer. It was somewhat awkward at first because everyone was always in his or her military uniforms so at times it appeared like a battlefield not a hospital. Most of the time as an officer walked into the room I saluted them, other times I flipped them off even though I did not know why, I think it might have been that part of me always wanted to do so but only now I was able to get away with it. Either action seemed to get the same reaction though, as everyone was just happy to see me moving. I had some more intensive therapy here they would also sit me up a short time every day so I could get used to being upright again. This was tough because almost immediately after they tried to sit me up my butt started to hurt. I would get light headed; my entire body quickly became fatigued, and started to sweat until eventually it just collapsed, but I couldn't do anything about it. When they thought it was enough or saw that I could not take it any longer they would transfer me to the bed again. Most of the procedures that were done at Stormont-Vail were also done here only by a different group of medical personnel. Once again a good number of them were also beautiful young women. I especially remember a few of them one whose name was Lea Grant. I remember her the best because beside her being sweet, and beautiful among other things she understood sign language so I would spend hours trying to communicate with her with what little I remembered from elementary, eventually we would further develop a sign language for which one of the male nurses named Eric would make a poster and place it next to my bed. Among the things it displayed were simple hand expressions to let the nurses know I was hungry, in pain, or had a dirty diaper, on this poster it also said in big letters "DO NOT TURN ON RIGHT SIDE." This was extremely important seeing how I had a large portion of my head without the bone to protect the brain and any pressure on my brain would cause more brain damage.

Besides the medical staff the base Chaplain would also come to see me, and my family just about every day. One day while he was there I began to vigorously scratch one of the pillows within my reach and my aunt saw this and thought I wanted to write something and although that was not my intention I did not object, so she got me a pen and something to write on. Despite having overheard the medical staff, and my family.

Even though I was already somewhat aware that I had been involved in some kind of severe accident I was still uncertain about the details as far as to what, when, and where. So I managed to write, "what happened to me?" He turned white and then stared blankly around the room for help. It was like he thought "this is even too tough for me." He talked with my aunt and eventually they told me that I had been shot in the head but left me with the unanswered questions of who had done it and why. More of my friends came to see me at this hospital, and although I could not interact with them in many ways some of them would stand next to my bed hold my hand and talk to me. It cheered me up to see them and despite what everyone thought I recognized all of them right away. My Aunt and Grandma, however, did not seem so happy about the visits as they did not know who it had been that shot me, so they looked at all of them as if they were the one that had pulled the trigger. Even though my stay here was shorter I remember more incidents than from Stormont-Vail. I recall that my grandmother, and aunt where almost always in the room, they would stay until late into the evening, and then walk to a nearby Ronald McDonald House where they were staying and come back early in the morning regardless of the weather which got pretty wild only leaving me alone in the room to go eat and to go to sleep. One time though while they were both eating lunch on a day that the nurses that usually took care of me were not there another nurse placed me on my right side and stuck a pillow behind me so I could not turn back face up. As he was turning me I felt like hitting him and yelling at him "Don't you know how to read" but I could not do anything so despite my struggle to turn over I could not manage to do so As I lay there the pressure in my brain got stronger by the second my head started to throb, my body started to sweat I even cried. I lay like this until my family members came back from their lunch, which I think was about forty-five minutes.

The therapists here, although not as funny as Jeff were also great the main therapist was a Major who I got along well with. Seeing that one of my biggest challenges was communication, and seeing how I still remembered how to write she devised a special pen, which consisted of a normal pen or marker with a large piece of foam around it so it would be easier for me to grip. This was extremely helpful as even though my writing was not very neat it was for the most part understandable and allowed me to communicate better and faster. It was early spring and anyone that is familiar with the weather in that region knows the kind of storms that occur there during that time of year. Often there would be storms nearby so severe with thunder and lightning that the medical staff would have to move my bed away from the windows. Seeing how my hand was tied to the bed railing most of the time and the bed had its controls there I would play with them all day and night sometimes putting the bed all the way up as high as it could, other times I would put my feet and head up so it would end up in a V shape, other times I would put the feet up and the head down or just keep playing with the controls. Finally somebody disabled the electrical controls. This was awful because now I had nothing to do to pass time. There were a lot of people on the medical staff whose names I do not remember but am very thankful to. There was this male nurse I believe a Captain who did something really nice for me see the NBA season was winding down, and I was a big Lakers fan, he found out and recorded a big game that they had. He then got a TV and VCR for me to watch the game on. I was so excited, but before I could watch it my body just gave out and fell asleep, even though I don't recall the game I do remember the thoughtful gesture. Eventually I was transferred over to the Department of Veteran Affairs and was transferred to one of their hospitals. A few days before I would be transferred, Lea showed up with a couple of flowers in a small glass, handed them to my aunt and told her they were for me and that she had dreamt that I was sitting up and talking to her. Everyone was sad to see me go and at the same time happy for me as I would be transferred to a Hospital in the Los Angeles area where I would be closer to most of my family and friends. I was nervous about going, what made it worse was that my aunt and Grandma had scheduled flights to go back home and wait for me there since they were not allowed to accompany me. It was the worst trip I have ever taken it would consist of me being carried on a stretcher onto on a series of hospitals on a plane that would stop at several cities to drop off and pick up patients sometimes leaving them overnight in different hospitals around the country. I don't know exactly how many planes or flights I ended up taking all I know is that I threw up numerous

49

times on every one of them as the motion would make me sick especially during take offs and landings. I spent the night in a hospital I believe to have been located in Denver, the next day I was then taken by ambulance to the airport where I would be loaded onto another plane on these occasions the ambulance crew were not the ones that would place me on the plane instead they had to hand me over to another crew in some kind of shuttle especially equipped and trained to load patients on stretchers onto these special. Planes. Planes, Ambulance, shuttle, and hospital pretty soon all became blurred, and I lost track of what was what. On one maybe two occasions I was among a group of patients on one vehicle waiting to be transferred to another and recall hearing that some of us were almost out of oxygen. My vantage point was not very good so I could not see exactly what was going on, but the tone of voice of the people that were administering the oxygen to us was one of concern as they spoke between them and told the people on the other end of the radio that the oxygen tanks were running out and would not be able provide all the patients that needed it much longer. Although I tried not to think about it and remain calm it frightened me to think that if we did not get more oxygen tanks I would be in a lot of trouble. Eventually they got us the necessary oxygen and onto the other vehicle. On one of the plane rides they had left my hand loose. It was a very long flight and I had nothing to do, not even play with the bed controls, so I looked up and there was a strap that went around the gurney above me, so I grabbed onto it and started pulling myself up to see. A little later one of the nurses saw me doing this and told me to stop I didn't, so he tied my hand down to the side of my gurney he tied my hand very tight. I assume that there was another patient in that gurney and if I continued to do so I might hurt him or her. This didn't matter to me though so every time the nurse that tied me up walked by I furiously flipped him off. Between transfers, headaches and throwing up I managed to get very little sleep however I could not stop thinking it was just a bad dream and that soon I would somehow wake up and everything would be the same as before the gunshot get up and go back to my life, my unit, and my work just like if nothing had ever happened.

Chapter Four

My Personal War Begins

After a terrible trip that felt a lot longer than the two days it lasted I Finally arrived at Sepulveda V.A.M.C. in North Hills California the week before Memorial Day 1993. At the time I arrived there was no one that I knew there, since I arrived in the early afternoon and my family had been told I would not arrive until later that evening. This was good though as this gave the nurses a chance to change my clothes and clean me up a little before my family arrived. Once they arrived they seemed to be glad just to see me alive, most of them had not seen me since before the accident so they did not know what to expect. Some of the younger kids such as my 2 brothers and some younger cousins seemed to be frightened, which of course is quite understandable. I was sagging down in a wheelchair, looked like a skeleton, and despite the nurses' best efforts my clothes, which were hospital pajamas (which always make you look sicker than you really are) were soaked with sweat, and smelled terrible. As if this wasn't enough I was hooked up to several tubes and hoses that also had some vomit on them. At first there seemed to be some reluctance on everyone's part to get close to me as they seemed to be stunned and were not sure that I recognized them. Well the first day the visit did not last too long as I was fatigued, and visiting hours were close to being over. Over the next couple of weeks a lot of people came to see me some mostly family members came daily and stayed with me in my room or accompanied me to exams and evaluations of all types, which were being done almost constantly. I was fortunate to have as many visitors as I did, usually my visits would start almost immediately after the hospital rules allowed it and lasted until visiting hours were over sometimes later as nurses would make exceptions, I was placed in the hospitals stroke-Rehab ward as my injury had conditions very similar if not identical to those of a stroke. Of course as you might expect with me being only eighteen I was by far the youngest patient there, this was beneficial to me, as all of the medical staff would treat me very kindly. All the patients were old enough to be my grandfather so the ones that could talk would say that I reminded them of their grandson and call me the kid. With several hours a day of bedside therapy I was getting stronger and apparently healthier every day. I still could not talk so the speech therapist came up with a few new more efficient ways for me to try to communicate. First of all, she brought a letter board that I would spell words out on, the problem with this method was that since I still did not have full control over my right arm, had so much to say and wanted to say it all at once I went so fast that no one could really understand. Then she brought this device that looked like a microphone that I would place on my neck next to my throat and when I would talk a robotic voice would come out of it, the fact that this worked not only made it easier to communicate but also meant that in all likelihood there was no major damage to my vocal chords and there was a good chance that I would possibly regain my speech once the tracheotomy was removed although no one could be sure until that time came. The doctors had to be sure that I was able to breathe well enough to breathe without it so when it came time they plugged it up first, and for the first time in months I heard my voice. At first it was a weak whisper-like sound, but it was better than nothing. In the meantime the staff would have me sit up longer and longer, once again I started in a standard reclining chair then moved up to a wheelchair with a high reclining back with head support, and full of pillows on the sides to hold me up. Gradually they removed the pillows and supports until I was able to sit in a normal wheelchair with nothing but chest restraints, and of course a protective bicycle helmet. I continued to receive bedside therapy every day. Eventually I began to weakly move my right leg the first muscles to come back were the ones that adduct the leg. On the bed and with my knee bent and I would bring it up from laying to the side to almost completely straight in front, but I was not able to hold the muscles tight for more than fractions of a second and my leg would just flop back down to the bed almost immediately this quickly improved and soon I was able to hold it in for extended periods and control it out again. Then the medical staff saw that I was strong enough to go down to the therapy clinics. Every morning I would wake up at about 6:00 am, after breakfast (which was still being given to me through the tube in my stomach) and morning hygiene, which was almost always given to me by the same two nurses (Addie and Marlyn.) Although all of the nurses were great Addie and Marlyn quickly became my favorite at least in the day shift. After they got me ready at about 8:45 am I was picked up by an escort that would wheel me down to the therapy clinics in the basement where I would generally spend most of the morning. Usually one hour in Kinesiotherapy with Neal, Beverly and the rest of the staff where they had me do many exercises. First so that I would start getting used to standing upright again, they would place me on a table, strap me down with a series of thick belts the first went across my chest, another at my waist, one more at about thigh level, and the last one slightly below my knees. Then slowly tilt the table up a few degrees and leave it in this position for a small amount of time. I felt like Frankenstein was just waiting to get hit by lightning so he could come back to life. With almost every session that passed they increased both the angle and the time but it was a slow process as I would often get dizzy and turn pale so they would have to bring me back down especially when the increase was a large one. There I would also work on my range of motion and flexibility, when the hour there was over I would wait for another escort to come and wheel me down the hall to Occupational therapy where despite only being scheduled to spend an hour I would almost always manage to spend the rest of the morning. Here I would work with Judy the therapist, and Tom a Vietnam Veteran who volunteered at the clinic. While we spent most of the time working on dressing myself, transfers, and basically anything else that would make me more independent, we also worked on fine movements, coordination and strengthening of the right arm and hand, although we weren't there to have fun we always managed to do so. I am not sure why, but Tom would often call me Mr. Trouble I imagine it was in part because I was the most energetic patient he saw all day. I started lifting weights using a pulley system they had in the clinic while in the wheelchair I would do numerous variations of movements that had similar effects to exercises such as bicep curls, triceps extensions, bench press, and many others. At first it was tough even with the minimum weight, but my right arm and upper body rapidly regained most of its strength and coordination. A short while later at the other clinic Beverly had me try to pedal a stationary bike that had been adapted so it could be used while sitting in a wheelchair. She also had me stand completely upright while tied into another device, which would not let me fall I loved getting this movement into my life again; however there was a problem with it. Since I did not yet have full control of my bladder I still had a urinary catheter. Sometimes with all the movement the hose would get tangled on something and yank it, which was severely painful, and caused it to disconnect therefore spilling the urine in the hose. Once my right leg was a little stronger they had me try to walk in the parallel bars and sometimes around the clinic or out to the hallway while Neal, Beverly or another therapist held me with a gait belt that was placed around my waist, but it seemed to be hopeless as my left ankle was so weak that it would regularly twist so severely I still wonder how it didn't break. In this clinic I would also lift weights here my favorite exercise was the lat pull down which is usually done with both hands, but I instead grabbed the bar from the middle with my right hand and struggled to pull it down. The first time I was barely able to pull down one or two plates, however after a few weeks I was pulling down about half the stack, almost pulling myself out of my chair. At least for me the time I spent in these two clinics was enjoyable and managed to cheer me up as it took my thoughts away from what appeared to be my cruel reality. After spending the entire morning in therapy it was back to the ward to eat lunch before going to speech therapy. For the first few weeks I did not receive a tray since I still had a feeding tube and a tracheotomy meaning the food could easily go to my lungs instead of my stomach after a few more weeks the doctors put a plug in my tracheotomy (which as I mentioned earlier allowed me to speak again.) Before they plugged it they did a series of X-rays, to make sure that all the congestion was gone and that there was no further need to suction my lungs. Then a few days later they decided to give me a chance to eat solid food, but first there was a procedure that had to be done. It was a test called a Barium swallow to see if I was able to swallow correctly. I had to swallow some liquid compound, the stuff I was supposed to swallow felt and tasted so terrible I could not swallow all of it and thought they were going to leave the feeding tube in and not let me eat until they repeated the test, but instead a couple of days after the test I received a food tray at lunchtime. When Lynn tried to feed me I did not attempt to swallow but instead let it fall out of my mouth, as it was too bland and soft. I did not like any of it, when I did not eat anything on this tray, which was all like baby food. Judy the head nurse contacted Dr. Wallis who was my main Neurologist. Her or her assistant gave the ok to order me a normal tray which I had no problem eating. I did get full rather quickly but enjoyed tasting, chewing and swallowing the food. Then at about 1:30 another escort would pick me up and wheel me to Speech therapy it just happens that the office I would have speech in was at the top of the biggest hill in the tunnels so the escort would get tired about halfway and I would have to help by spinning the right wheel then the left wheel while he pushed, on the way back I usually loosely dragged my hand along the rim and my foot along the ground in order to slow the chair down Before I went back though I spent an hour in this room with Cathy, and another lady whose name I don't remember practicing my speech through tongue and mouth exercises. In Speech therapy I did more than just learn to talk again. It was a place where I would frequently have tests on my ability to deal with society. There were also a number of voice strengthening exercises, where I would scream as loud as I could. Since my loudest scream sometimes could barely be heard the therapist taught me that in order for me to be louder I had to extend the vowel sounds as well as use my stomach muscles when I spoke. One time the Speech therapist came down to Occupational therapy where I blew bubbles at Tom in order to strengthen and train the stomach muscles that I was supposed to use when talking. Tom was great about it as he normally was about everything else I did to him. All he cared about was helping me get better. As a matter of fact when I first started to weakly straighten my leg he would put his hand in front of my foot and tell me to kick his hand and this motivated me to kick harder and harder. This time he sat across a table from me as I blew bubbles in his face, I guess I know now why he called me MR Trouble. After Speech therapy it was back to the ward at about 4:00 PM the day nurses left, and the next shift took over, usually there was Norma, Hazel, Soli, Enid, Theresa, and Lynn who often also worked other shifts. Usually after dinner there would be entertainment and activities such as Bingo or other activities a typical 18 year old would not find very entertaining, but I guess I wasn't a typical 18 year old anymore, as this experience had changed my life completely and had no choice but to enjoy these activities. Usually organized by Veteran's organizations like American Legion, Disabled American Veterans (D.A.V) or Veterans of Foreign Wars (VFW) and a few others, these were quite fun. The events were sometimes held on our ward 22C or on another ward in Building 2 and patients would come from other buildings to play. To make it fair for every patient, though they were held in different places. Most of the time though they were held at the nursing home (Building 99), or at the recreation center (Building 23). When they were in another building or ward there were several of us that would wait for escorts to come get us and roll us across the hospital most of the time through the tunnels that run below the enormous hospital campus. On occasions when it was nice outside they would take a shortcut through one of the parking lots drop us off and come back at the end of the activity and wheel us back to our ward. In 22C there were several of us that usually went to all the activities, at least three of us even carried lucky Bingo cards in the bags that hung from the back of our chair. First of all, there was Johnny Ordaz an elderly World War II Veteran who not only had suffered several strokes but also had Parkinson's disease, diabetes among other things but because of his positive attitude was well liked and better known as Johnny O by everyone from nurses to therapists throughout the medical facility. He and I developed a great friendship; he was an enormous inspiration to me and other patients, as he did not let his condition bother him. Of course he was not delighted about being paralyzed and wheelchair dependable, having uncontrollable movements all day, and numerous other medical conditions for which he had to take medications, but no matter how bad he was feeling he always had a smile on his face and was always joking around. Next, Suren was a middle-aged man who I think had worked as some kind of radiology technician in that same hospital for a number of years prior to suffering a severe stroke that left him in a similar condition as Johnny and I. to name a few of the problems the strokes or in my case the accident had left each of us with at least half of our bodies paralyzed, failing eyesight, poor coordination, a speech impediment, uncontrollable movements, lack of memory, and many other medical conditions, which needed to be constantly monitored. Despite all this on a couple of occasions when the escorts took too long the three of us who already knew the way would sometimes get restless and go on our own we would propel our wheelchairs down the hallway by grabbing the handrails with our good hand and pulling then when we got to the end of the hall the two of them who had more use of one of their legs would use that in combination with their good hand to continue to propel their chair until they reached another handrail, I on the other hand developed a crossing over method where I would alternate to spin both wheels with my good arm. Now it was time to go down to the basement this was a real challenge, as we would need to get on the elevator. A big challenge it was, but we somehow managed then it was time for perhaps the biggest challenge of our journey the tunnels. These were so lonely they looked and felt abandoned sometimes almost haunted, not to mention all the slopes and hills in the underground labyrinth. It was the closest thing to a roller coaster we could go on at the time. Even though we knew how to get where we were going we would sometimes get confused and struggle to find the correct path. Once we arrived we had lots of fun sometimes we would win, others we would just get our refreshments and have a great time. Even when we won the winnings per game were only a quarter or a $1 coupon to buy whatever you wanted from the hospital cafeteria or store. When we got back to our ward the nurses were worried about us and scolded us for having snuck off, but we didn't really care. Then it was time for our nightly doze of medications and off to bed we went. even though I probably had the least number of medical problems I was still taking a lot of medicines some were to prevent me from having seizures, others included sleep aids, muscle relaxants, and pain medications. after a few weeks I was transferred out of my private room and into a mini ward inside a bigger ward. The room held sixteen patients four beds per row. Although this was not my favorite sleeping arrangement it had its benefits first and foremost Johnny was in the bed next to mine and by his bed there was a window I could almost see out of the little that I could see was the sky or at least the reflection of the moon and the stars as it appeared on the window. Suren was still in a private room down the hall. Regardless of the room I was in whether it was a private room, or the big 16-person room nighttime was always terrible. There were no visitors, and I often spent a large portion of the night awake either from being awakened by severe pain or by all the noise around me, as there were always P.A. announcements about emergency situations or other noise. During the time I remained awake I could hear other patients screaming, moaning or banging the trapeze against the pole it hung from. In case you don't know the trapeze is a metal triangle handle that hangs overhead from a metal pole. This was not the worst though as sometimes I could not fall back asleep not due to the noise or my pain but instead from the awful smell of human excrement that swept across the entire ward from the cleansing of one of the patient's colostomy or from the changing of someone's diaper. Some of the nurses who usually worked this shift were Linda, Eva, and Yolanda who was not the nicest of people, and that is quite understandable seeing as this was the time that patients usually caused the most problems, seeing as most of us could not sleep through the night without waking, and while awake had nothing to do but call the nurses. While some patients had to have something tended to others just wanted attention, and would call for the nurses every 5 minutes, when they did not come quickly enough we would try to get their attention one way or another way or another. It seemed to be a different patient or two every night. None of us were free from this, I had my share of nights in which I could not sleep and drove the nurses crazy I particularly recall one night when I was still in my private room my leg would spasm and turn over on its side every few minutes and since I had to sleep with Night splints to prevent foot drop this caused great pain in my hip and knee so I would call the nurses who after many times decided to prop my leg with several pillows to prevent it from twisting. First though they stopped coming as quickly so I grabbed the trapeze and started banging it against the pole. This brought them in but when they left a few minutes would pass before my leg got messed up again. Eventually Yolanda came in grabbed my left hand and slapped me with it. I will never forget that night not only because of the slap but also because I had always wondered why the other patients were so annoying. When I found myself in the same position I could not believe it, but now I understood why or at least I could relate to the others when they did not let the rest of us sleep. From that night on they would fill my bed with pillows to keep my leg in place although this didn't seem to help much though as my legs would spasm uncontrollably, flinging the pillows from the bed leaving me with the same problem. Since there was nothing I could do, and the nurses could not stay all night in my room I just had to learn to tolerate it.

Chapter Five

The Struggle Continues

As time passed I became more and more accustomed to life in my condition however I felt useless, like life was not worth living I was battling depression and had contemplated suicide almost every day since arriving here at this medical center, I guess the thought had been there since the accident, but my mind just wasn't clear enough to put together the details of how. Now I began to see a way and even planned how I was going to do it. See on the ward there was a staircase, which the hospital staff used to get around quickly some days in the little free time I had I would sit in my wheelchair by the door just waiting for it to stay open long enough for me to get to it after someone walked through it. Although many walked in and out of it they were always in a hurry so no one noticed that I was there it opened dozens of times but would always quickly snap close too fast for me to get a hand in and roll myself down the stairs. On a couple of occasions I managed to partially grab the handle only to have it slip through my fingers, eventually I would get tired of just sitting there, and go do something else like watch TV or talk on the phone.

During my stay at this medical center there were many changes in my life almost daily. Most changes severely affected me; the majority of changes were due to new accomplishments such as once again being able to feed myself, partially dress myself, regaining most control of my bowel and bladder, and wearing normal clothes instead of hospital pajamas. My life was also immensely affected by many events; perhaps the most memorable was for my 19th birthday when Addie, Marlyn, and all the other nurses organized a birthday party for me. One of them printed banners that said, "Happy Birthday Lenin," and hung them all over the ward; my family and some friends came to celebrate my birthday. We went out to a courtyard where we took pictures, laughed a while and had a good time. This to me was very important as it reminded me that I still had a whole life ahead and should not give up no matter how arduous my situation appeared to be. Although many of these events had a positive effect on my life, there were others that made it more difficult or just turned it upside down. First, there was the break up with my girlfriend. As you can imagine letting go was difficult, but I felt it wasn't fair to her to be stuck waiting for me to get better when in reality I knew I wasn't going to anytime soon. All the death and disease that surrounded me was not making life any easier either, it seemed like everyday someone else I knew would pass away as a matter of fact while I was in my private room the man in the room directly in front of mine died of stomach cancer, the following morning I saw the nurses had placed another gentleman in there and I believe he had a heart attack and died a few days later. Then there was a week this happened over and over again as I would see new patients in that room every few days. Once I had already been transferred to the big room there was a series of about ten days when every day the person that was placed in the bed in front of mine had a stroke or heart attack and either died or had to be transferred to Intensive Care where they would die shortly after either way I never saw them again, this usually happened in the early morning or late at night. There were times though that I would leave for therapy in the morning only to come back that afternoon and find that there was a different person in that bed, and although I got pretty used to it and understood it wasn't my fault that everyone that was placed in front of me passed away quickly I started feeling like if I was bad luck or something, to top it off Johnny and other patients would tease me about being bad luck to be in front of me. Johnny would say laughing how the day before he wanted to die he would ask the nurses to place him in the bed in front of me. Besides these deaths I would always hear stories about patients in other buildings and wards passing away When Judy the occupational therapist left it hit me hard after all thanks mostly to her I had regained almost full movement in my right arm. Although I could tell that she did not fully want to leave she was moving to Minnesota due to personal matters. Despite being replaced by another great therapist (Betty Lang) who I already knew, it was not the same since I was already comfortable with the way Judy did things. At first after she left I didn't want to spend as much time at this clinic. I kept going though and since Betty and Judy had worked together with me in the past we pretty much continued with the same routine. Tom was also still there. Betty would sometimes also ask Tom for input on how I liked to do things as he had worked with me a lot more than she had. For some unknown reason at least unknown to me the nurses who I was used to getting me ready every morning were also changed, Addie and Marlyn were no longer assigned to be my primary nurses. Instead it was usually Mary Lawton an elderly black nurse who had a reputation for being mean and strict. Yeah at first I thought she was mean, seeing that she did not spoil me as much as the other nurses and didn't like her very much, but over time I got used to her way of doing things. After a while of dealing with her she did not seem so mean, as a matter of fact I grew very fond of her. There was also a payphone in the hallway almost directly in front of room 228 the private room I was first put in. Sometimes in the afternoon after speech therapy when I had no visitors and there were no entertainment activities with the money I won in Bingo I would call most of my friends, of course this was when it was available since it was often used by other patients such as Suren, Johnny and of course MR. Pollock a blind elderly man who almost every night after dinner would wait for a phone call from his wife. They would usually talk for hours. While the phone was busy I would usually stay in the dining room watching TV while someone played the piano or talking with my visitors. Sometimes though there was a psychologist by the name of Robert Saray who would come talk to me. At first we would talk there in the dining room but of course sometimes there were many numbers of distractions. On those times that there were too many distractions and as our conversations became more of a psychologist talking to a patient rather than your everyday conversation he would take me to his office. It was located all the way on the other side of the hospital; the walk was so long that sometimes by the time we got to his office there was not much else to talk about. What I remember most about Robert is that the ties he wore seemed especially funny to me. The first time he went to see me he had a Mickey Mouse tie and although I don't recall exactly what other ties he wore, the thing I do remember was that most had cartoons and were all silly, unique and made me laugh. I mean here we have this elegant doctor with a Mickey Mouse tie, but I guess this was part of his plan though as this made him more approachable to patients like me. We discussed just a few topics in these sessions, at the time I thought the sessions weren't very helpful, but now I realize they were more helpful than I thought. It gave me someone relatively close to my age to talk to about whatever I wanted. Even better was the fact that everything I said was confidential and would not affect our relationship at all, a lot of times I used Robert to let out my frustration which was something I could not do with my friends or family. While I felt that I could talk to them about most things, and it would help me release some pressure I knew that there were also things I could not say without hurting their feelings. Most of the time after our sessions Robert would take me all the way back to the ward, but on at least one occasion I convinced him to leave me in the downstairs lobby where there were also a few payphones from which I would talk with some friends a while before going back up to the ward. Usually nobody else was there. Sometimes I would just go down to the lobby not to use the phone but just to be alone where no one would bother me and sit there in deep thought; this deep thought was rarely but on occasion disrupted by voices of what resembled to be Shadows. In reality they were the voices of doctors or visitors just passing by. Everyone that passed either did notice my presence or ignored it as I did theirs. The same characteristics that made this lonely place ideal for sinking deep into my thoughts also made it spooky especially when it was dark outside. The next big blow came the time that Dr Wallis's assistant told me that an HIV test I had had a couple of days earlier came back positive I immediately freaked out, and asked the doctor how that could be possible if I took many precautions to avoid those types risks before my accident. He suggested that it could have been due to the blood transfusion I had had while being operated on, this really scared me. Another possibility was that of a mix up in the lab, so he ordered a retest as is usually done with all positive HIV tests. Another two days passed before I got news of the results, they seemed eternal as I agonized every moment thinking enough is enough it could not be that I would have that kind of luck on top of the shooting to also have been infected with HIV. He then informed me that it had been a mix up that caused a false positive; it was like a huge weight had been taken off of me allowing me to once again breathe calmly, and my blood to circulate again. I had not told anyone as I figured everyone on the medical staff knew anyway and did not see any point in telling my family and friends, even less after knowing that it was a false alarm. I never told anyone except Robert a few days later and that was because he mentioned something about it on the way to his office, apparently he already knew everything. There were always parades and barbecues on hospital grounds as Sepulveda is a huge city like complex with roads and many buildings. The reason I bring this up is because a funny thing happened during the 4th of July barbecue. Seeing how I still had both the tracheotomy and the feeding tube in I was not supposed to be eating or drinking anything however the escort that was pushing me around was never made aware of this and offered me a hotdog and a glass of punch which I gladly accepted. That afternoon when it was time for the nurses to give me water through the feeding tube. Using a syringe Lynn pulled out some of the liquid in my stomach like they always did before injecting anything. When this red liquid came out and she got really scared, as did Addie and Marlynn who were also in the room, seeing their faces I began to smile and the grin on my face let them know what had happened. When they saw it was just punch they found it humorous but were also upset and told me I shouldn't have done that since I was not allowed to eat or drink anything until I had the doctor's permission. On 22C there was also a patient by the name of Mr. Howtzer who had also suffered a severe stroke, among other illnesses he had a problem that often caused him to urinate blood. I mean it wasn't that I would watch him pee, but like most of us he also had a catheter and his urine bag hung in plain sight. The urine inside was always red so I assume it was bloody. What I most remember about him though is a comment I heard him make to my step dad, see they were talking about smoking and he told my step dad that even though he had suffered from emphysema for a good number of years he still smoked four packs a day, my step dad then asked him why he kept on doing it if he knew it was that bad for him he replied" " my last 5 doctors have told me that if I didn't quit smoking it was going to kill me," he paused short of breath then continued " you know what all five of them are dead and I'm still here shows how much they knew." I don't know if it was a joke or if he was serious, all I know is that he wasn't alone in the love of cigarettes. There were a number of patients that I would see going outside the buildings to smoke even with their oxygen tanks strapped to the back of their wheelchairs. I remember one in particular rather well, although I don't recall his name his image is unforgettable I saw him sitting on a loading dock smoking with an oxygen tank on his chair and oxygen tubes on Although he was just one out of many I saw in this situation he stood out because he held the cigarette not with his hand but rather with a metal hook he had. My brother Jason, who was10 at the time would sometimes come by in the afternoon and stay with me until someone came to pick him up in the evening. He would usually go with me to speech therapy, although he was just a kid having him there was of great comfort, there were a few times when he found me crying just depressed as can be I would talk to him for a while, and this made me feel better. The nurses and some of the other patients soon knew who he was and befriended him, one patient even taught him how to play a song or two on the piano. On a day that he did not come the escort had not shown up and it was almost time to leave for speech therapy seeing how I was confident that I knew the way I decided that I would go on my own, everything was fine until I got to the bottom of the big hill which I tried to climb but despite using all my strength and momentum to push the chair part of the way up before I could do anything I would find myself rolling back down toward the bottom. I must have tried about ten times getting further up with every try but still no success, then it hit me not to try to go up front wards but rather in reverse this way my leg could help me. I struggled to make it up and almost quit trying but I finally made it. That was quite a work out, I was exhausted but after therapy was complete I did not bother to wait for an escort instead I wandered off on my own when I got to the hill I was hesitant but still went down it. As my chair sped up I tried using the same technique I used when going with an escort (dragging my hand on the rim to slow it down) but it burned so I removed my hand, I completely lost control of the chair and the low speed I was going at probably 10-15miles per hour at most, felt like if I was in a car going well over 90 however I did not try to stop the rim because this would have almost certainly hurt my hand and turned my chair completely sideways causing it to flip over. I felt the chair start to shake and needed to do something quickly, and although it hurt my hand it seemed to be my only option so once again I dragged my hand along the rim. This time I applied more pressure causing my chair to slam against the wall slowing it down as it scraped against it. I did this repeatedly and finally using this technique I managed to slow down enough for me to regain control of the chair, this was the first and last time I went to speech therapy without someone pushing me. Despite having almost killed myself on the way back it was not the last time I returned from there without someone helping me as I found the ride down the hill very exciting. Sometimes after being at the Nursing Home Suren, Johnny, and I would race back to the ward. Although it didn't really matter to us who actually won it was still a race I wanted to win so I would do my best throwing caution to the wind I would speed down hills, around turns on one occasion I lost control of the chair and could not slow down going down a small hill, I saw the end wall straight in front of me as I usually did on this hill but this time I could not slow down enough to make the necessary turn and slammed into the wall almost at full speed. Fortunately the front most part of the chair was the foot rests, as the right footrest went through the wall and the chair came to a stop. I did not feel anything at that instant. I guess because of the Adrenalin, but when I got back to the ward my right big toe was in tremendous pain. It was swollen and red, but I did not let anyone know for a couple of days, not even in therapy even though when I would put weight on it the pain was almost unbearable I made faces and yelled every time I stood so they soon noticed. When they asked I told them it was something up on the ward, surprisingly they did not make a big deal about it and call the ward instead they put ice on it and treated it like any other injury. Some of the nurses also noticed but when they asked how it had happened I told them it was in therapy from walking so much or else they might not have let me out of their sight again. Once again to my surprise they did not make a big deal about it they just gave me pain medication when I told them it hurt. A couple of weeks passed before my toe was fine again. As for my visits even though more friends from high school came to see me most of them were curious one-time visitors and my visits diminished as time passed. Some friends from Kansas also found me. One of them a soldier whose room was next to mine in the barracks called me from his new station in Hawaii his last name was Johnson I think. Although we did not talk much because I could not talk very well yet just knowing that he cared enough to find out where I was, and call meant a lot to me. Another friend Michelle came out from Kansas on her vacation and stayed at my parents' house for about a week, she spent most of her time at the hospital with me. Unfortunately her friend Shauna did not come with her this time though as I would have liked to have seen her too.

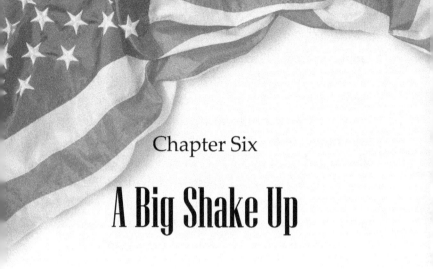

Chapter Six

A Big Shake Up

As terrible as my situation was with every day that passed I was becoming more and more accustomed to my new life and starting to enjoy certain aspects of it. I was becoming well known to patients, patients' families, and staff. I also had a lot of personal belongings such as clothes, pictures, and a few colognes next to my bed. Some of my old friends continued to visit me, and occasionally with permission from the doctor I would go on pass, sometimes it would only be a few hours in the afternoon, other times I would spend the entire the weekend at my parents' house. Although it did not feel like home anymore at least it was a change of scenery and environment. We would even go out to eat or go shopping at nearby stores; once again I thought the worst was behind me when on January 17,1994 at about 4:30 am I was suddenly awakened when the ground violently began to move. It kept vigorously shaking for approximately 15 seconds, which seemed like an eternity; at first I had no idea what was happening then having experienced several earthquakes I realized that this was another. It was the Northridge earthquake that with a magnitude of 6.9 that felt like if it was at least 7.5 it devastated most of the Los Angeles area especially the San Fernando Valley. I guess what made it feel worse was the fact that the epicenter was only a few miles away, I was Awakened not only by the movement, but also by a thunderous ruckus and the screams of many patients including Johnny. I grabbed onto the trapeze as Johnny yelled, "hold on tight Mijo" as he used to often call me, as the ground continued to move everyone figured out what was going on. Over the noise of windows rattling, tray tables falling, and beds slamming around I heard other patients as they screamed for the nurses, as they normally did. Only this time it wasn't their usual pointless screams; these had the sound of panic in them. Johnny and I looked at each other, the look on his face said it all he was scared as was I but still we did not panic, after all what could we do anyway. Instead we reached over our heads and managed to find the cord for our overhead lights but when we pulled on them the lights did not go on. The room for that fact the entire ward was in total darkness and time seemed to stand still. Then I saw the flickering light from the nurses' flashlights just outside the room for a few moments in which seconds appeared to be minutes then I heard and saw Linda. The other nurses on duty that night followed closely behind. They tried to keep everyone calm as they examined the ward for gas leaks, but I could tell by the look on their faces that they themselves were terrified. Johnny, who did not appear to be scared anymore, and I were talking to the other patients trying to keep them calm. Some emergency lighting came on before the hospital's generator kicked in Even with the dim lights we were still pretty much in complete darkness. Through the dark all I could see was the beams of light coming from the flashlights as they glimmered through what appeared to be smoke that had accumulated. At least from my point of view the place looked and felt like a graveyard. From what I could tell the ground was wet or at least I could hear how the nurses' shoes splashed in the water and as the wheels on our chairs rolled through small amounts of water on the ground. There was also a faint smell of gas that grew stronger with every moment that passed. After a couple of minutes the generator kicked in and power was restored. By this time the nurses despite being completely perplexed with everything going on had somehow managed to get all the patients that could get into a wheelchair into one and wheel all of us to the area where the elevators and stairs were located, but the elevators were unsafe to use. We needed to take the stairs, which were only a few feet away, the nurses then pushed us over there where I along with many others were quickly but carefully carried down by nurses and people like Tom and Neal who had come to help evacuate the hospital. I know there were many more brave, unselfish people that came to help but I can only clearly

79

recall these two as I was in shock and pure amazement that the same stair case I had once wanted to kill myself in would somehow be used to save my life. As the ground continued to shake we were taken out to the parking lot outside building 2. As morning neared I watched as these heroes ran back in to get more patients out over and over until every patient was out. Some were not able to get out of bed, they were somehow brought out in their beds. Then some of the staff went back in to get some blankets to protect us from the early morning frost. Meanwhile the ground continued to rumble with more and more aftershocks. Immediately before each one I could hear, as there would be a loud sound similar to a lion's roar then a fraction of a second where everything was in complete silence. A while later when the sun was coming up my family who lived a few minutes away came to see if everything was ok. It was then when someone pointed out that building 3 the building where the Intensive care Unit was had a large crack down the middle which you could clearly see through to the other side, I imagine there were many deaths in that building that day as most of those patients were on life support of some kind and even though the power outage had only lasted for a few minutes I think this could have caused the machines that were giving them life support to go off causing death. While we sat there in the parking lot freezing until the early morning I once again wondered if everything I had just lived was real or if my mind was playing tricks on me; I was wearing my helmet and some hospital Pajamas so I could not wait to get somewhere warm, but then someone, I don't know who handed me a blanket which somewhat shielded me from the chilly temperature, yet I was still freezing and concerned as I did not know where Johnny and many of my friends were. Sometime after 7 am buses began to arrive and take us away. There was a lot of confusion in respect to who would be going where. Somehow amid the confusion Johnny, Suren, and I managed to get loaded onto the same bus. We were taken to the West LA Veteran's hospital, which was further from the epicenter and had not been affected as much by the earthquake or its aftershocks. There we were given necessary medications and something to eat, while we were there the aftershocks continued. At times they seemed to be getting larger and more frequent, everyone was scared especially since the wing we were in was under repair and one of the stronger aftershocks knocked down several pieces of the ceiling that were already loose as part of the repair. All of us stayed there a couple of hours until they decided that there were too many patients for them to handle. It took them a while to decide what to do with all of us. At about 10 am some of us were loaded back onto a bus. Suren was one of the patients that stayed in West LA, Johnny and I along with many others were taken to Jerry L. Pettis Memorial Hospital a Veteran's hospital in Loma Linda also known as the Loma Linda VA. By the time we arrived it was early afternoon, we were given something to eat, necessary medications, and a room in the respective ward that we were assigned. I was placed in

2 Southeast (2nd floor Southeast wing) the stroke Rehab ward. Many of the others including Johnny were placed in other wards including downstairs in the nursing home (1 South). This trip had been a terrible one too but not nearly as bad as the one from Kansas to California or at least the adrenalin that was rushing through my body did not let it feel like it. Once I arrived at 2 Southeast I was greeted by Audra the receptionist and some of the nurses that were waiting to check us in. I was wheeled to a room right across from the nurses' station where there were four beds three of which were empty. In the only occupied bed was my new roommate Tim West, I recall he had a white mustache and was balding, yet appeared to be only in his late fifties or early sixties which was considerably younger than the people I was used to being with. He appeared to be completely healthy; in fact despite seeing him there I did not figure he had any kind of medical problem so severe that he needed to be in a hospital. Although my first impression of Loma Linda was favorable, as it looked beautiful and different from any of the other hospitals I had been to. Once again it was rather difficult to get situated here despite its beauty. First of all, I was once again far from my friends and family since Loma Linda is about an hour and a half away from the San Fernando Valley where they were all located (not to mention I had no idea where I was). Furthermore, some of the existing patients looked at all of the new patients from Sepulveda as outsiders who were not welcome. I was also concerned about the whereabouts of Johnny,

as I had not seen him since we were still on the bus that brought us from West L.A. Another thing that caused me difficulty during the first few days was that I had to be in Hospital Pajamas all the time since I lost all the personal items I had at Sepulveda, these also included a brand new electric wheelchair that was given to me when the V.A. awarded me 100% disability rating. I was told that all my stuff was in all likelihood lost or damaged during the earthquake, and that I should file a claim for losses. I waited a few days to see if it somehow showed up. After a week when it didn't show up I immediately filed a claim. Once again all of the nurses here were very nice to me despite being overloaded with work. Deborah Walker a young black nurse was my favorite nurse at first. Debbie was in her early thirties and quite attractive, she would always come when I called. As time passed with no news of Johnny or anyone else from Sepulveda I was afraid that besides my physical possessions I had once again lost everyone I knew. Aside from going to therapy and to the pay phones, which were just around the corner, I hardly left my room for fear of getting lost. In this hospital there was a phone by each bed however since all of my calls were long distance unless I had a phone card, which I did not it was practically useless, and I could only receive calls. Besides the phone this room also had a TV, which I needed to share with MR. West or whoever was in the bed next to me, but regardless it was the first time I had a TV in the room since I was in the private room at Sepulveda where I had one brought in but only used it to watch VHS movies, as it did not have cable MR.. West always told me to watch what I wanted though. Well after a couple of days I had to start physical therapy, and occupational therapy every morning, and once again occupational therapy was right after physical therapy, and just down the hall. Although this hospital did not appear to be made up of a series of Buildings as far as I could tell, it was the nicest of the hospitals I had been in. On the second floor not only was the floor, which housed the stroke rehab ward but also had the dental clinic, psychiatric ward, barbershop, bank, and many more things. What I remember the most was that right in front of the physical therapy clinic was the hospital gift store and right next to it was a huge cafeteria. On the first floor was the nursing home with a pond and lots of ducks outside. Also located on this same level were the prosthetics department, many other administrative offices, and an emergency room. On the third floor there were the postoperative wards, and if I'm not mistaken on the fourth floor were the cancer wards, along with operating rooms.. There were sets of elevators one at each end of the building. Every time the elevator doors opened a voice would tell you what floor you were on and which direction the elevator was going. I was impressed once again as the only thing I remembered from the elevators at Sepulveda was that they made a loud buzzing sound every time they reached another floor. Loma Linda also looked better taken care of with clean, freshly painted walls, and signs everywhere to let patients, staff, and visitors know where they were.

This single building had everything a patient could need. I'm confident that the other hospitals also had these things, but I never saw them as I was not in a good enough condition to wander around them like I did here. The best thing here though was the staff. The physical therapy team was made up of Anna a Hispanic woman in her early thirties, Annette another Hispanic woman in her late twenties, Flora an Egyptian woman in her early thirties, Norma a white woman in her late forties, Rosemary a Polish woman in her mid thirties, and Dennis a white man in his thirties. The head of the department was Jack a white man in his mid-forties. Rosemary would be my main therapist; she had long blonde hair down to her waist and was always laughing. On one of my first visits to physical therapy an elderly doctor by the name of Dr. Sterling was there along with Rosemary, and the rest of the rehab team. Dr. Sterling was a physical rehabilitation specialist and had come in especially to evaluate my condition. After a few reflex tests and some range of motion I was taken to one end of the parallel bars, with a gait belt around my waist and a therapist nearby, everyone's eyes were on me and one of them asked me if I was able to stand up, so I grabbed the parallel bars and with help pulled myself up to standing. When I tried to walk my ankle kept on twisting. When Dr. Sterling saw this he immediately told the others that the first thing I needed was an A.F.O (a brace that supports the ankle and foot) on each foot. I tried on a standard AFO that they had in the clinic and although it was uncomfortable as it was not molded to my foot it provided my left ankle the stability it needed for me to walk without twisting my ankle. A few days later. I was fitted for a pair of my own, Joe the person who made the braces placed some surgical tube down my shin and wrapped it with a wet cloth with plaster on it. He let it dry a few minutes then I nervously watched as he brought out his saw and cut it off, he did this for both legs and a few days later he brought back two braces that were supposed to fit my feet perfectly, but of course there were some minor adjustments that had to be made where the plastic needed to be bent out in order for it not to put too much pressure on a single spot. A few days after he came back with my braces, overall the braces were great, they were black like I requested and had the exact specifications that Dr. Sterling had ordered, the right one had a hinge at the ankle otherwise they appeared to be identical. When I wore them I felt like a robot, but they gave me a sense of balance and security, so I soon began walking in the parallel bars and around the clinic. Seeing as I did not need the right one to stand or walk, and it was the most difficult to put on I stopped wearing it after about a week, I kept working hard in therapy in fact I spent most of the day in the physical therapy clinic. I did not get tired; I don't know if I could say the same about Rosemary and the others. Not only did I go in the morning but also I was often the last patient to leave before lunch and the first one back afterwards. I spent as much time in this clinic as they would allow. In the meantime people were appearing in my life again. My parents moved to Corona, which is only about a half an hour away from Loma Linda, most of the nurses from Sepulveda, were working there now although not in a fulltime position, I was still glad to see them when they did. A couple of weeks later Mary Lawton worked on 2SE, and boy was I glad to see her especially since she told me that Johnny was downstairs in the nursing home then wheeled me down to see him. When I saw him again it felt great, I wanted to jump out of my seat and hug him. Here in Loma Linda there was another nurse also named Mary who I became very fond of. Mary Jones usually worked from 5 am to 2 pm she was also black in her early to mid-thirties, between the two Mary's, and Debbie I was given a shower every day. Mary Jones, who worked almost every day, would come in and offer showers to everyone. Since most of the other disabled patients would refuse to have a shower would go to my room and say, "hey kid lets go I'll give you a shower." On her days off either Mary Lawton, or Debbie would come in a little later in the morning and give me a shower. I was one of the few patients to get a daily shower, as everyday instead of fighting the ones that refused to shower the nurses would clean them up in bed. At about noon everyday it was time for lunch, seeing as I did not like most of the food that the hospital provided me Rosemary would usually buy me something. Most of the time she brought me a hamburger, other times she would buy me something at the cafeteria, sometimes she would get there earlier than usual and would buy me donuts or something else for breakfast.

We spent a lot of time together especially after Dr. Sterling's second visit. In this visit he suggested I try a new kind of brace called an R.G.O. or Reciprocating Gait Orthosis, after discussing it with the other doctors there he ordered it. Joe ordered the mechanical parts to it a couple of days later came in to cast me for the braces. I thought he would only need to cast my legs once again but this time he also cast my upper torso, a few more days passed before he brought the apparatus in. It was like a full body brace that consisted of two knee high braces, each with a metal bar that ran along the outside and attached it to some mechanical device that I was to wear around my hips. This device also went attached to a chest plate, once again there were a few adjustments that needed to be made to the plastic parts of it. It was almost impossible to get in and out of it so unless they were major ones they were left alone. Once it was finally adjusted it helped teach my body learn how to walk again by swinging my left leg all the way through using the little movement I had at my hips. When I first got this device I did not have the balance to use it outside the parallel bars, but with dedication and hard work both from Rosemary and myself I progressed out of the parallel bars to walking with a hemi-walker, to walking with a large base Quad cane or four point cane, at first I walked while she pushed herself backward on a little stool with one hand holding onto me and with the other pulling my left foot through when it didn't clear the ground. Then she would just walk backwards in front of me, we walked at least a couple of hours a day. We must have walked up and down every corridor in the hospital from the first floor to the fourth floor. Sometimes it seemed as if I was her only patient. Soon I progressed to a small base Quad cane even to a single point cane but preferred the small Quad cane as it gave me more freedom to use my good hand for other things and did not interfere with my right foot's motion.. As you can imagine the time that we spent walking we also did a lot of talking. She became my best friend, my confidant, almost my psychologist. I felt completely safe with her. During the time I spent there I was also seen by a psychiatrist as once again I suffered from an intense depression, but Rosemary was always there for me. She was more helpful than any psychiatrist, psychologist or medication.

Chapter Seven

At The New Battle Zone

Life here at Loma Linda was changing rapidly, and although I went down to visit the nursing home from time to time I saw less of Johnny and others from Sepulveda every day. One day when Mr. West had already gone home they put a patient by the name of William Curtis in the bed next to mine, I believe I seemed to recall Bill from either 22 C or the nursing home back at Sepulveda. He was in his mid-sixties, and as we got to know each other he told me about his life. Like Johnny and many others this man told me lots of stories about wars they had been in or other events that truly inspired me make the best of my life instead of giving up. Years earlier he had suffered a stroke that left him paralyzed and in a nursing home unable to take care of himself. It was there in that nursing home he met his wife who he married during a TV newscast before being separated due to their health conditions. Like Johnny he was also a World War II Navy veteran, he used to be a singer but now suffered from frequent seizures and a slight speech impediment. Besides that not only was his left side paralyzed, but also had some permanently contracted muscles and due to a lack of therapy and movement could not straighten his leg more than halfway This made it almost impossible for anyone to stand him up so he spent a lot of time in bed, this included eating in bed a lot of the time which only seemed to worsen his condition, we tried not to let our situation affect us and joked around a lot. On occasions when he was up and out of bed he had a one handed wheelchair (a wheelchair in which one of the wheels has two rims, each one controls one wheel allowing the person in it to control both wheels from the same side.) He was even teaching me Morse code, and in his slurred speech he would try to teach me the alphabet. Sometimes in the afternoon we would spend lengthy periods of time in the lunchroom, he would go through and explain each letter for example saying, "S is dit, dit, dit." He would do this for every letter until I could repeat it back to him, I was not very interested but knew that not only did it made him feel good but also did him good to be out of bed besides it was not like there was much else to do. Later in the evenings there were often Bingo games or other functions down in the nursing home I tried to attend as many as I could however I was not always aware of them. Furthermore I was not supposed to go out of the ward by myself but when the nurses were busy with something or someone else always managed to do so anyways. Even when there was no Bingo I often went down to the nursing home visit Johnny, other patients, and some nurses that worked there. Abandoned by their families, and with terrible medical impairments many patients would patiently sit there waiting anxiously for someone, anyone to visit them, while others yelled for no reason whatsoever. Then there were the ones that yelled for the nurses with what appeared to be excruciating pain. While the majority of these patients needed medical care that could probably not be administered outside of this environment, there were quite a few patients like Johnny who were stable mentally, and physically but could not take care of themselves so their families just left them there hardly ever going to visit them. Most of the nursing home's patients' favorite way of relaxing was to go out by the pond and feed the ducks. They would often save their slices of bread from all of their meals so that they would have something to do. On occasions I would wander around the rest of the hospital I would go around the second floor up to the third and fourth floor where Mary Jones had once taken me to see a young cancer patient by the name of Tim Brown. At this time of day most of the hospital was desolate but nowhere as much as these last two floors. Their lonely halls reminded me of the Lobby back at Sepulveda and also provided me with a wonderful place just to sit there and ponder about how at least to my previous expectations my life would never again be normal. Still depressed I once again considered suicide, but then I thought about all of the things I had already gone through and how if I gave up now all my efforts would have been for nothing. On one of my many trips around the hospital I was going too slow when going out of an elevator and one of the wheelchair's front wheels got stuck in the groove the door slides through. I sat there trying to get out, but it was useless no matter how hard I tried the chair did not budge I was just spinning the wheels in place while the elevator door repeatedly slammed into my wheelchair and the voice from the elevator kept on repeating" Second floor going down, second floor going down." It was frightening as it was late and almost no one was around, after about ten minutes I thought I might have to wait until morning before someone would see me. Finally as I began tiring, sweating intensely, and giving into this thought a janitor passing by helped me out of the mess I was in. A few days later the same thing almost happened again only that this time I was prepared, and as soon as the wheel fell immediately placed my right foot down on the ground and pushed up while turning the wheel, liberating myself again. These were two of the more mentionable incidents in all my travels through this hospital. It was now late spring of 1994 and the NBA playoffs were on. I enjoyed watching them and still cheered for the Lakers even though they were not too good at the time. Then another player caught my attention it was Reggie Miller from the Indiana Pacers who I thought was amazing and quickly remembered watching him when he was playing for UCLA as I had planned to do one day, and once again became a Reggie Miller fan. Along with him I began to like the Pacers, which shocked me as having grown up in the Los Angeles area the Lakers was the team I had always adored. One day another man was placed in an empty bed in the room, he was Mr. Ross a big time Lakers fan but after a few games and a couple of weeks of talking about basketball I convinced him to stop rooting for the Lakers, and he began to cheer for the Pacers. Roughly three weeks after his arrival he was transferred to a room down the hall where I would visit him whenever I got a chance. I only visited him a couple of times since about a week after he got transferred he passed away from a heart attack. Besides everything I saw and heard in the nursing home, and at the other hospitals, here I also saw shocking medical conditions I had never seen or heard of before. A large number of patients were outpatients that were admitted and placed under observation for a couple of days or spent the night before a surgical procedure or an exam, which required an extended amount of time. Although most of these patients were in what appeared to be good health a couple had some major complications while they were there. The one I remember the most was a patient with an Italian last name which I do not recall who was placed in the bed in front of mine he was thin, in his mid-thirties and appeared to be in excellent health. His first day there everything appeared to be fine then on the second day all of sudden late in the afternoon during the nurses shift change he started to violently shake and move his arms and legs all over the place, it looked like they were going to fly off of his body I had never seen anything like it so I grabbed the call light and pressed it repeatedly when the nurses did not appear I got out of bed and into my chair and went and got one of the nurses after I told him what was going on he came running to see exactly what was going on. He just watched as the patient's body continued to shake for about five minutes, and as saliva poured from the side of his mouth. The nurse explained to me that he was suffering what was known as a grand mal seizure and that there was not much he could do and that it was best to let it run its course. He then called the doctor and let him know what had happened, I however could not see how that could be I thought that there had to be something they could do, but apparently the nurse was right, and it had not been as bad as it looked. The following day he appeared to be just fine and checked out a few days later. I don't recall seeing or hearing about him again. Besides paralysis the most common sight here was probably amputations as there were a lot of diabetics and patients with seldom seen diseases, and skin conditions. There were all kinds of amputees, but the majority of them were patients with one full length leg and the other amputated below the knee as doctors always try to save that joint as it is supposed to make it somewhat easier for the amputee to get back to walking once they get a prosthetic leg. All other kinds of amputations were also seen; there were patients with both legs amputated below the knee. There were patients with no legs at all or one leg amputated above the knee and one below. On a good number of these patients I did not even notice that they had amputations until I saw them remove their prosthetic leg or legs in the therapy clinic. They walked around with limps, used canes or crutches but after all we were in a rehab ward. There was this one man who was a diabetic and had another disease, which caused him to have chronic infections leading to him losing both legs. One was amputated while I was a patient there, I remember seeing him one day at therapy, I think he had lost his first leg not too long before and was walking with a walker when he sat down he took off his prosthetic leg and handed it to Joe so he could take a look at it. I guess it needed an adjustment. I overheard him tell Joe that he wanted both to look and feel similar. I did not know what they were talking about but the next time I saw him would be about four weeks later, meanwhile I heard therapists, and doctors talking about how he had gone through surgery but for some reason I had little idea that they were going to cut off his other leg. When I finally did see him again he was in a wheelchair talking with Joe who was fitting him for a new leg. Joe had also brought him his other leg, as well as a few choices for his stump socks (cloths similar to socks that amputees wear in order to achieve a better fitting artificial limb and protect the stump from sores, and infection). There were many amputees but none in as bad a condition as this elderly man who in one way or another had all four limbs amputated.

I only saw him a couple of times one time as a nurse pushed him down the hall, and another in a customized power wheelchair. His situation shocked me, but I tried not to stare as this might make him feel uncomfortable but from the little that I was able to see and what I found out he was just a trunk with little stumps for legs as both had been cut at about mid-thigh and a stump on one arm which had been amputated below the elbow due to his Diabetes, and infections. While the other arm was full length, he too had a metal hook since he only had two or three fingers remaining on that hat hand, as the rest had been lost in some kind of accident while he was in the military. Disability was not limited to the patients though as there were some staff members that were paraplegics and amputees, but perhaps the one that stands out the most was Toni a social worker who was frequently on the ward and had her office on the way to the therapy clinics. She was a young woman in her mid twenties who had no arms and did everything with her feet. If I remember correctly she was born with only stumps for arms, on one occasion as I was in her office the phone rang and thinking to myself" should I ask her if she wants me to get it" I watched as she calmly slipped one foot out of her shoe grabbed the handset between her toes put the phone to her ear and began talking. There was another time when someone needed her to sign something and she told them to drop it then slid her foot out of her shoe, asked the person for a pen grabbed it and signed the paper with her foot handed (or footed) the pen back. She then put her shoe back on and continued with what she was doing. The fact that most impressed me was that she did all this without losing her balance. After seeing all this I felt somewhat fortunate about my condition, however I still had a hole in my head so they would have to operate. The surgery needed to correct this was called a Cranioplasty, from what was explained to me by Dr.

Esparza (one of my many doctors), was that there were a couple of ways of doing it. The first being to make a plate that would fit the hole perfectly and screw it onto my existing skull, the other way of doing it which to me sounded better involved getting my bone fragments from the bone bank in which they should have been placed into right after my gunshot. Grinding them up, and mixing them with a special kind of glue, then spreading this mixture over a titanium mesh, which would be screwed onto my skull allowing the bone to grow and heal itself just like any normal fracture would. Before they could proceed with this option though they needed my bone fragments, which they could not find so they decided to go with the first option. By choosing this option it meant that a special plate had to be created to exactly fit the opening in my skull, so they took an assortment of x-rays and a CT scan of my head. As the operation neared I was unsure about how to feel on one hand excited about not having to use that dumb helmet anymore, I also foolishly thought that there was a possibility that once I had the operation my body would somehow regain movement as if this whole thing had never happened. On the other hand though I was concerned that something might go wrong, and I would end up worse than I already was. Then I met Charlie an ex-marine who had fallen about fifty feet from a water tank somehow hitting his forehead shattering his skull right above his nose and causing severe brain damage. His injury was very similar to mine but because of the location of his injury surgery was not an option so in all likelihood he would need to not only endure the cosmetic disfigurement, but also wear a protective helmet for the rest of his life. It was then when I realized how fortunate I was that I had that possibility and the little concern I had about the surgery quickly dissipated. In the weeks prior to the surgery in addition to all preoperative tests a plethora of X-rays, and CT scans were taken. Dr. Kujikaro the neurosurgeon who would be operating and whose name I probably am misspelling came to see me a few times to manually measure the opening you would think that he would have an easier time getting the measurements from a computer generated image than from him taking measurements with a measuring tape, but this is how he chose to do things and who could argue. The surgery was in the early summer of 1994. The morning of the surgery, which was scheduled to begin at about 7:00 am, I was awakened at about 4:30 am. I was placed on a gurney and wheeled up to the surgery room but before surgery my head needed to be shaved and washed with a special disinfecting soap. While they prepared me for surgery I was freezing especially since besides a hospital gown I was not allowed to have anything on not even a blanket. Due to the cold and nerves my body trembled as I felt when they lathered up my head and carefully shaved every hair off of it. After they finished they took me into the operating room. As I stared up into the operating lamps I heard them talking about my arterial pressure, and heart rate then they placed a mask with the anesthetic over my mouth and nose, everything started to fade. The lights got dimmer their voices got softer, I was frightened, but wanted to stay awake and fought against the effect of the anesthetic. The next thing I knew was when I saw a nurse and asked her when they were going to operate. She just looked at me smiled and said, "it has already been done." It turns out the surgery which lasted several hours was already complete, and I was in the recovery room lying in a bed which I believed to be the gurney I was originally taken to the operating room on. I then looked around and saw my mom who confirmed that they had already operated. Although I didn't think I needed it I was then taken up to the third floor for postoperative care where doctors wanted me to spend four to six weeks recovering. The very next morning Rosemary and Doris a student that was helping out in the clinic came to see me, later that day Mary Jones also came by as a matter of fact the visits kept coming for the entire period of time I was on the third floor my visitors included some of the many doctors, nurses, and therapists that had worked with me in the past few months. I could not wait to get back to 2 Southeast and continue with my rehabilitation. My head was bandaged; they would remove the bandage every few hours just long enough to clean the area around the wound. I had hundreds of staples that seemed to be a train track going from my forehead to the back of my head. A couple of days later I was feeling fine, so I escaped the ward and went downstairs to the other floors to see Bill, Johnny, and let everyone know I was doing just fine. Although everyone was glad to see me, they angrily told me to go back upstairs finally, one of the nurses gave me a push all the way back.

Actually I was feeling fine the day after the operation, incredible what an eighteen year old body can endure, I mean less than 24 hours after having my head sliced wide open, having 14 screws drilled into my skull and closed back up I was already feeling fine. After about four days convinced that I was fine the doctors transferred me back down to 2 Southeast, once there I was placed in the same bed and resumed my normal activities such as physical and occupational therapy. Once on 2Southeast I had more visitors there was my Aunt Vilma and her family, my parents, brothers, and grandparents. It was still summer, and one of the physical therapists Anna brought her two children in on occasions to keep me company. Marcos and Melissa were younger kids but just like with my brother the time we spent together was unforgettable. Here at Loma Linda I would also be allowed to go on pass most of the time it was to my parents' new house, but my aunt Alba and her husband would also take me out to shows and movies. I continued with therapy and after nearly two years on October 28,1994 I was discharged from the hospital. I thought I would live with my parents while continuing with therapy and my other rehabilitation, but I guess they had other plans. See while I was in the hospital my mom thinking it was in my best interest and something I wanted to do had used my money to purchase an apartment in Colombia for my grandparents to live in the problem was that since we did not have all the money she had to get a loan and both the loan, and the apartment were in my uncle's name. Seeing this and how my parents lived in a two-story house and they both worked all the time I could not live with them anymore convinced it was the right thing to do I reluctantly agreed to go live in Colombia and put the apartment in my name or sell it. On November 5th after only a week or so since being discharged from a twenty-month hospital stay I was on a plane headed overseas to live with my grandparents until I solved this issue.

Chapter Eight

Away From Home

Traveling to Colombia was difficult even though my aunt Alba went along in case something unexpected came up during the trip. The flight to Bogotá where we spent the night at one of my grandfather's sister's house lasted about eight hours, we finally arrived in Armenia (a smaller city inside Colombia) our final destination the following day, my aunt spent a couple of weeks there then returned home. The plan was for me to stay until either I sold the apartment or put it in my name, which shouldn't take too long. This, however, took longer than I expected. I spent most of the time with my uncle who still lived with my grandparents at the time and took me almost everywhere he went. He often took me to my grandparents' farm, sometimes we would walk through the crop fields together but seeing how as it was uneven dirt and narrow walkways which were often obstructed by branches as you can imagine made it a tough terrain to conquer so other times he would go by himself and look over the crop fields to see what there was to sell while I stayed either in the car or at the main house then he would come back and go over the books with the farm's administrator to see what had been paid and what still remained unpaid. When we were ready to go workers would usually load the car with coffee or other crops, we would then go into town and sell whatever was meant to be sold. Despite it being terribly uncomfortable and difficult the walks through those fields were very helpful, not only did they help in regaining some more of my balance but also in helping me deal with my depression as besides keeping me busy they would bring back joyful memories of when I was a little kid running through them. There were times when we went to banks in the city's downtown, in order to claim the money my mother would wire me, as well as to pay the mortgage on the apartment. Talk about a rough terrain, most of the time we would have to park in a parking lot a few blocks away and walk through the crowded streets only to get inside the bank and have to negotiate stairs and wait in long lines. At least inside it was quieter and cooler, I however did not always feel like going with my uncle so on occasions I stayed home with my grandparents and watched TV. On the news there was always tragic stories about kidnappings, car bombs, and massacres. When it wasn't by one of the country's many guerilla groups or drug cartels, it was nature's fury which caused havoc whether it was heavy rains that led to landslides which covered entire villages, and major roads or pests that destroyed large crop fields and harvests that devastated both the local, and national economy. Whatever the cause social conditions there were frightening. Although everyone I had contact with treated me wonderfully and went out of their way to ensure I was comfortable wherever I went it wasn't long before I realized that this was not the place I wanted to live. I needed to get back to the United States, but it proved to be difficult and seemed to be too late because while trying to make life more manageable I had made some costly adaptations to the apartment, and it seemed like every day I was making more. I had also made quite a few friends besides my cousins, most of whom I got along great with despite not having had any contact with in over a decade. Before I knew it I had been sucked in by the culture and was living a comfortable life there. I was getting therapy from a family friend who had become an occupational therapist when her son was born with some paralysis. Therapy had a completely different approach and was not as intense or demanding as the ones in the hospitals, but it still helped a great deal or at least gave me something to do and look forward to everyday. In these sessions I met several Colombian soldiers, and police officers that had also suffered on duty accidents and had similar medical conditions, but unlike me had very little support from their government. In the meantime I also attended many healing conventions all over the country, and despite not being fully convinced I did always get my hopes up that some kind of miracle would happen, and I would regain the functions that I had lost as a result of the gunshot, only to be thoroughly disappointed after every single one. There was also the time I went into what was a pool with Natural thermal water that supposedly had some kind of healing effect. The water came from a thermal spring in the nearby mountain range. Nestled between mountains partially covered by fog and full of trees and other vegetation the place was beautiful. Along with this, the mist that rose at every point where the water relentlessly fell into the pool made it look mystifying but to my disappointment did not heal me instead it seems like the only thing that happened that day was that I badly scraped up my feet from walking barefoot. In an effort to fit in and make everyone happy I often went to church often; besides therapy and all these religious events, I joined a gym and bought a 25 pound dumbbell which I would lift in my free time which I usually had lots of. During the period of time I lived there in the late 1990s I lived in a good area of the country that was not severely affected by most of the catastrophes or widespread violence. I did, however, see poverty like I had only seen on TV. I felt confused I wanted to help but at the same time I wanted to run back home to the United States. Feeling trapped not only by the social conditions but also by being physically unable to get on a plane and go back to my country. Emotionally weak and unsure if I would be well received, seeing how at least in my mind most of the people I thought I would always be able to count on had turned their back on me. Unwilling to risk losing the acceptance and support of those around me, who with open arms despite all my limitations had made me a part of their lives and shown me the affection I was denied by those I expected it from I just endured, which seemed like the only thing I could do. Accompanied by my grandmother I did however come back to the United States for about a month during the spring of 1995. We spent a little over half of the time at an uncle's house near Orlando and two weeks or so with my Aunt in California, hesitantly staying at my parent's house only for a couple of days to be closer to the Loma Linda VA where I had appointments on three consecutive days in order for the VA to confirm my eligibility for benefits. During those visits I went around the hospital, and on the first day I was able to see Rosemary, and a few others, Mary Jones however was on vacation so I was not able to see her, which was disappointing. When I asked about all the patients I remembered I was told that most of them had died, while a few others had gone home. So many patients had died I was scared to ask about Johnny, and Bill, but when I did someone told me that they thought that they had been transferred somewhere else but did not know where. Eventually though one of the nurses that used to work at Sepulveda told me that she thought Bill, and Johnny might have been transferred back to the nursing home at Sepulveda, I wanted to see them, so when I went back to my aunt's house I asked her to take me to Sepulveda to see if they were truly there but did not have the time to go seeing how a couple of days later I had to return to Orlando where I would depart for Colombia. Even though I was not totally convinced that they were at Sepulveda the fact that I was not able to go see Johnny, and Bill before reluctantly going back to Colombia compounded with my frustration of not being able to see Mary Jones really upset me. I did, however, stay long enough to see a few friends from high school, and my old neighborhood that came over to my aunt's house. I also got to watch that year's NCAA basketball Championship that was won by UCLA. While living with my grandparents my grandfather had several debilitating strokes, he would get noticeably better after going through various treatments, only to have the next stroke take him back to the same or worse condition. In early 1997 seeing possibilities of further rehabilitation in the United States my grandparents moved to Florida where he passed away after several months when he suffered yet another series of strokes. Living alone now I saw myself forced to hire a caretaker, it needed to be someone I trusted, so I hired the lady who worked taking care of the apartment for my grandparents, she was the logical choice seeing how she already worked there and had been around the family for over fifteen years. With my uncle now married he was no longer able to take care of my errands, so I became friends with a couple of cab drivers who would take her and I to the banks, stores, and wherever else I needed to go. A few weeks after she started working for me I began dating her oldest daughter (Milena) who I would go on to marry in July of 1997. Once she gave birth to our first child (Britny) in November of 1997 the first thing on my mind was getting the two of them back to the United States where we could have a better life. We did all the necessary immigration paperwork for both of them in the first 2 months of 1998. After receiving a large sum of money from the V.A I paid for the apartment, transferred it to my name and was finally able to move back to California in March of 1998. Thinking back the biggest thing that kept me in Colombia for so long was the fact that before I was married regardless of all the support I had been shown by people in Colombia I was not sure that there was anyone that I could count on to stay by my side and whose support and acceptance I would not lose if I expressed my desire to move back to the United States. Although without doubt the toughest years of my life, I wouldn't say that the time I spent in hospitals, and living in Colombia was bad, but merely different from what I was familiar with, and a learning experience I needed to go through and learn from. Not only did I for the most part get to spend the last few years of my grandfather's life by his side, but also completely experienced another two cultures, (as I consider living in the VA hospitals a different culture altogether.) I was also now married and had a four-month-old daughter; however I don't know if any of these things would have otherwise happened if it were not for the nearly twenty months I spent in hospitals, and close to four years I lived in Colombia. When I got back to California one of the first things I did was go to the hospitals where I had lived to see how everyone was. I went to Loma Linda first where once again I was able to see Rosemary and the rest of the physical therapy staff, however when I went to 2 Southeast I did see a lot of the nursing staff who told me that Mary

Jones had called in sick that day I felt cheated since every time I went she was not there. Not convinced with the answer I had received four years earlier about the whereabouts of Johnny, and Bill I asked everyone again finally down at the nursing home again I was told that they had been transferred back to Sepulveda along with all of the remaining patients that were transferred from there after the earthquake. This answer convinced me more than the one that I was previously given, however I still wanted to see Mary, so I went back a few days later, another nurse Naomi who was friends with Mary told me that she had Recently passed away from breast cancer. This was devastating, especially since I did not get to thank her for everything she had done for me while hospitalized. Having lived most of my life in areas close to the Sepulveda VA I wanted to stay nearby so I purchased a house not too far from there which made it possible for me to frequently visit Johnny and Bill. On my first visit to Sepulveda I saw that a lot of changes had been made, a new building had been built in the parking lot we had been evacuated to after the earthquake and most of the old buildings despite still standing had been converted to offices and outpatient clinics. Except for those patients in the nursing home no one lived in the hospital, I went through some of the buildings before I ran into Addie, Marlynn, Lynn, and a lot of other staff members I remembered from five years earlier. After the initial burst of excitement from seeing each other again one of the nurses informed me that Johnny had suffered a heart attack and passed away not too long before, but that Bill was still there in the nursing home. Although not entirely surprised by Johnny's death it did leave me in a state of severe sadness, in large part because I couldn't recall exactly when the last time I saw him was. Then I came to the conclusion that at least he was not suffering anymore, and whatever our last moment together was it had been an enjoyable one. I also knew that just as I would never forget him he had not forgotten me. I then went to see Bill who despite almost four years having passed and having added some weight was still the same Bill, as I had known in the past. One thing that really made me happy was the fact that when he saw me he immediately recognized and remembered me. Over the next seven to eight years I visited Bill whenever I was near, or in the Sepulveda VA complex on an appointment (probably once every couple of months) I was glad to see that he was hanging in there, despite not getting any better or being able to be out of his bed as often as before. He still seemed to be as coherent as always. The times I visited him we would spend a lot of time talking mostly about his wife, the nurses, and the people he met through his ham Radio. One time as I walked in with my wife by my side he was sitting in bed with his ham radio set up in front of him, it sat on what I believe to have been a hospital table. He pointed to the wall in front of him and showed my wife and I postcards from people all over the world, which he had been communicating with. He told us that one of the nurses had pinned them up on the wall in front of him so he would see them every day. He looked like a child opening gifts on Christmas day with everyone he told us about he got just as excited as with the previous ones. It made me sad to think that he was so alone in the world that every time I asked him if anyone else had been in to see him he would tell me the same thing and that was that his son was too busy with work but had told him he would be coming to see him the following month as soon as work got a little lighter. I think he rarely or never went to visit, as a matter of fact while Bill and I were living together (over a year and a half) I only remember seeing him one time. Even though a nursing home is not a very child appropriate setting, on at least one occasion I took my daughter in to meet him, he seemed to enjoy seeing her. Unfortunately due to personal and family obligations I was not able to visit him as much as I would have liked. I had several conversations with Bill most of them would be filled with laughter; however the one I remember most was the saddest one. The last time I went to see him in late spring 2006 he was lying in his bed quieter than normal not laughing or telling jokes like he usually did. We talked for a while, but this time it wasn't like our previous conversations then one of the nurses brought in his lunch tray as I was preparing to say bye his eyes begged me to stay until he finished, so my wife and I went to a visiting area where we waited for him to eat when I felt like he was done I went back in while my wife went to the car to wait for me. He was done so we talked some more he told me he had done everything he wanted and was ready to go any day now, inside me I knew it would be the last time I would see him so I tried to prolong my stay, but it was almost time to go pick up the kids from school so I had to leave. Before I finally left though deep in thought I quietly stood by his bed for a few moments, grabbed his hand thanked him for his service to the country, and his friendship, bent down and gave him a kiss on the forehead. As I walked out of his room I felt my throat choke up with emotion and my eyes start to water. When I got to the car almost unable to talk from crying I told my wife that I knew it was the last time I would see him. Over the next several weeks I called him a few times before I went on vacation with my family, as it was summer. When I returned I had an upcoming appointment at Sepulveda, so I called to see if he wanted me to take him anything. As soon as I dialed his extension I was transferred to the operator who just told me that Mr. Curtis was no Longer there, I then asked to be transferred to the nurse's desk. I asked the nurses on duty one of them told me that he had been transferred to the West LA Hospital, but none of them knew who I was so they could not tell me anything else. A few days passed and I called the nursing home again and when I asked for Mr. Curtis once again no one would give me information I then somehow spoke with Lynn who knew we were like family and informed me that he had been transferred to the VA hospital in West LA due to some complications and that he had passed away in his sleep a week or two earlier from what she believed to have been a brain aneurysm. Once again not surprised by the news, and although saddened by the loss of another great friend I was relieved to know he was not suffering anymore. I knew he had not forgotten me either and that I had been there for him in difficult times. In the nearly fifteen years since my accident I have had many difficulties from which I've learned a great deal. I have seen large amounts of death, and disaster (to the extent that all of my true friends from my teenage years are now dead). At the same time I have also met many wonderful people who have helped me enormously and have also been fortunate enough to be able to help many people going through a bad time of their own. On top of that I have seen firsthand why the United States is the country that whether or not they admit it every country in the world envies and almost everyone wants to live in. I say this because at least in my experience, regardless of my situation or location the U.S government has always been there to help and has provided generations of my family and many others the opportunity for a better life. I have also learned that it does not do anyone any good to show your affection for somebody after they are dead. Besides everything previously mentioned I've also been diagnosed with many other conditions and diseases since the gunshot. I don't want to bore anyone with all the details but some of these are a seizure disorder, Posttraumatic stress disorder, Depression, and even mild Dementia. I look at all these diagnoses as just labels and do not allow them to have a major effect on my life. What does have a major effect on it is my paralysis, since I can't just make my body move just by making my mind think I can move. My paralysis has taken away most of my athletic ability and fitness I once worked so hard to achieve, and any chance

I had of participating in professional sports, which I am confident I would have. I also suffer from frequent falls having fallen through tables, and chairs, one time even falling head first into a wall. In the time since my accident I have seen great improvement in my physical condition and although still paralyzed with frequent pain, and many other bothersome conditions live a good life that doesn't have anything to envy from anyone else's. In fact if I could go back in time knowing what I know I can't think of too many things I would want to change. I've also seen that no matter who you are life is always trying to hit you with adversity and in most cases it will hit you one way or another. I've also seen what makes a person who they are is how they react to getting hit. Through this book I would first like to thank all of the past, and present Service men and women of the U.S. military for their service to the country. Then not far behind all those people like nurses, doctors, therapists who provide the military, and others in need with essential support Others I'd also like to give a special thanks to all those individuals I mentioned. Furthermore, to those of you that I came in contact with but did not mention you also have my gratitude, but on top of that please accept my apologies but in the time since my accident I have had too many friendships abruptly ended to recall everyone's name. Although I have not given up on regaining more movement I have learned to live with my condition and along with my family try to make the best of it. Since I still love sports I try to guide my children down the path I did not get a chance to complete. As far as all the people previously mentioned, as I said before I can only imagine that all the patients I knew from Sepulveda except for Suren who I have seen along with his wife once not long ago are now dead. I still call Rosemary, and Tom from time to time just to say hi. They are both doing fine, I see Neal whenever I go in for therapy at Sepulveda where I occasionally also see Linda and other nurses. Last I heard Addie, Hazel and Soli retired. Although I haven't heard anything I imagine Mary Lawton also retired seeing how from what I heard she was already close to retirement fourteen years ago. After snooping around I found Betty who works at the West LA VA and almost didn't recognize me when. I went to see her. I was hoping she could tell me how to get in contact with Judi Rodgers, but she had no idea where she was either; however she was the one that helped me get back in contact with Tom who is helping me look for Judi. As for the people back in Kansas, despite my efforts to contact some of them I have not been able to and pretty much lost all contact with the medical staff from both hospitals. I have had some contact with a few friends from the army and others in Kansas I also keep in touch with Michelle. As for the guy that shot me I heard he was charged with assault, sentenced to something like three years in a military prison and dishonorably discharged from the Army. To him you know who you are so I won't mention your name and although I'd like to, I can't say there are no hard feelings but if it is any consolation. I have read all of the incident reports several times and realize that it was an accident. Another reason for writing this book was to help those in similar situations cope and to let them know that no matter how bad it looks you shouldn't give up. I find this especially important now with the great number of soldiers coming back wounded from Iraq and other places the US military no longer has any business being. If this book can inspire at least one person to keep fighting when it seems they are up against impossible odds or if it prevents one family from abandoning a loved one facing a terrible situation then it was worth writing so please let me know. I hope you enjoyed my story and there is more to come and if you have any comments feel free to send an email to info@LeninPatino.com